ENERGY POLICIES, POLITICS AND PRICES SERIES

ENERGY PRICES: SUPPLY, DEMAND OR SPECULATION?

ENERGY POLICIES, POLITICS AND PRICES SERIES

Nuclear Power's Role in Generating Electricity
Perry G. Furham
2009. ISBN: 978-1-60741-226-7

OPEC, Oil Prices and LNG
Edward R. Pitt and Christopher N. Leung (Editors)
2009. ISBN: 978-1-60692-897-4

OPEC, Oil Prices and LNG
Edward R. Pitt and Christopher N. Leung (Editors)
2009. ISBN: 978-1-60876-614-7 (online book)

Dynamic Noncooperative Game Models for Deregulated Electricity Markets
Jose B. Cruz, Jr. and Xiaohuan Tan (Editors)
2009. ISBN: 978-1-60741-078-2

Energy Prices: Supply, Demand or Speculation?
John T. Perry (Editor)
2009. ISBN: 978-1-60741-374-5

Worldwide Biomass Potential: Technology Characterizations
R. L. Bain
2010. ISBN: 978-1-60741-267-0

ENERGY POLICIES, POLITICS AND PRICES SERIES

ENERGY PRICES: SUPPLY, DEMAND OR SPECULATION?

JOHN T. PERRY
EDITOR

Nova Science Publishers, Inc.
New York

LIBRARY OF CONGRESS CATALOGING-IN-PUBLICATION DATA

Energy prices : supply, demand or speculation? / editor, John T. Perry.
    p. cm.
  Includes index.
  ISBN 978-1-60741-374-5 (softcover)
  1. Fuel--Prices--Forecasting. 2. Energy policy. I. Perry, John T.
  HD9560.4.E54 2009
  338.2'32--dc22

                                                    2009028448

Published by Nova Science Publishers, Inc. + New York

CONTENTS

Preface   **vii**

Chapter 1   Speculation and Energy Prices: Legislative
                  Responses   **1**
                  Mark Jickling and Lynn J. Cunningham

Chapter 2   Commodity Futures Trading Commission: Report to
                  Congressional Addressees   **23**
                  Government Accountability Office

Chapter 3   Regulation of Energy Derivatives   **103**
                  Mark Jickling

Chapter 4   Commodity Futures Trading Commission Trends in
                  Energy Derivatives Markets Raise Questions about
                  CFTC's Oversight   **111**
                  Orice M. Williams

Chapter Sources   **133**

Index   **134**

PREFACE

A lucid answer to the question of what causes energy prices to often widely fluctuate is hard to find. Is it supply, demand, speculation, manipulation, fear, price gauging by energy distributors or refiners or some hideous combination of all the above? This book provides basic information to try to solve this riddle.

Chapter 1 - While most observers recognize that the fundamentals of supply and demand have contributed to record energy prices in 2008, many also believe that the price of oil and other commodities includes a "speculative premium." In other words, speculators who seek to profit by forecasting price trends are blamed for driving prices higher than is justified by fundamentals.

Chapter 2 - Prices for four energy commodities—crude oil, heating oil, unleaded gasoline, and natural gas—have risen substantially since 2002. Some observers believe that higher energy prices are the result of changes in supply and demand. Others believe that increased futures trading activity has also contributed to higher prices. This report, conducted under the Comptroller General of the United States' authority, examines trends and patterns in the physical and energy derivatives markets, (2) the scope of the Commodity Futures Trading Commission's (CFTC) regulatory authority over these markets, and (3) the effectiveness of CFTC's monitoring and detection of market abuses and enforcement. For this work, GAO analyzed futures and large trader data and interviewed market participants, experts, and officials at six federal agencies.

Chapter 3 - After the collapse of Enron Corp. in late 2001, that company's activities came under intense scrutiny. Much of its business consisted of trading financial contracts whose value was derived from changes in energy prices. Enron's derivatives trading was largely "over-the-counter" (OTC) and unregulated: little information about transactions was available. Trading in energy derivatives rebounded after a post-Enron slump, and much of the market remains unregulated. This "regulatory gap" strikes some observers as dangerous for two reasons. First, the absence of government oversight may facilitate abusive trading or price manipulation. A June 2007 report by the Senate Permanent Subcommittee on Investigations concluded that excessive speculation by the Amaranth hedge fund, which failed in 2006, had distorted natural gas prices. Second, the failure of a large derivatives dealer could conceivably trigger disruptions of supplies and prices in physical energy markets (though the effect was minor in the Enron case).

Chapter 4 - This a testimony of Orice M. Williams, Director, Financial Markets and Community Investment, before the Subcommitte on General Farm Commodities and Risk Management, Committee on Agriculture, House of Representatives.

In: Energy Prices: Supply, Demand …   ISBN: 978-1-60741-374-5
Editor: John T. Perry   © 2010 Nova Science Publishers, Inc.

Chapter 1

SPECULATION AND ENERGY PRICES: LEGISLATIVE RESPONSES

Mark Jickling and Lynn J. Cunningham

SUMMARY

While most observers recognize that the fundamentals of supply and demand have contributed to record energy prices in 2008, many also believe that the price of oil and other commodities includes a "speculative premium." In other words, speculators who seek to profit by forecasting price trends are blamed for driving prices higher than is justified by fundamentals.

In theory, this should not happen. Speculation is not a new phenomenon in futures markets — the futures exchanges are essentially associations of professional speculators. There are two benefits that arise from speculation and distinguish it from mere gambling: first, speculators create a market where hedgers — producers or commercial users of commodities — can offset price risk. Hedgers can use the markets to lock in today's price for transactions that will occur in the future, shielding their businesses from unfavorable price changes. Second, a competitive market where hedgers and speculators pool their information and trade on their expectations of future prices is the best available mechanism to determine prices that will clear markets and ensure efficient allocation of resources.

If one assumes that current prices are too high, that means that the market is not performing its price discovery function well. There are several possible explanations for why this might happen. First, there could be manipulation: are there traders in the market — oil companies or hedge funds, perhaps — with so much market power that they can dictate prices? The federal regulator, the Commodity Futures Trading Commission (CFTC), monitors markets and has not found evidence that anyone is manipulating prices. The CFTC has announced that investigations are in progress, but generally manipulations in commodities markets cause short-lived price spikes, not the kind of multi-year bull market that has been observed in oil prices since 2002.

Absent manipulation, the futures markets could set prices too high if a speculative bubble were underway, similar to what happened during the dot-com stock episode. If traders believe that the current price is too low, and take positions accordingly, the price will rise. Eventually, however, prices should return to fundamental values, perhaps with a sharp correction.

One area of concern is the increased participation in commodity markets of institutional investors, such as pension funds, foundations, and endowments. Many institutions have chosen to allocate a small part of their portfolio to commodities, often in the form of an investment or contract that tracks a published commodity price index, hoping to increase their returns and diversify portfolio risk. While these decisions may be rational from each individual institution's perspective, the collective result is said to be an inflow of money out of proportion to the amounts traditionally traded in commodities, with the effect of driving prices artificially high.

This report provides basic information and analysis on the issue of commodity speculation and summarizes the numerous legislative proposals for controlling excessive speculation. It will be updated as events warrant.

OVERVIEW

Are oil speculators the messengers bearing bad news, or are they themselves the bad news? The Commodity Futures Trading Commission (CFTC), which regulates speculative trading in energy commodities, has found no evidence that prices are not being set by the economic fundamentals of supply and demand. Many analysts agree, arguing that long-term supply growth will have difficulty keeping up with demand. Others, however, believe that changes in the fundamentals do not justify recent increases in energy prices, and seek the cause for soaring prices in the futures and derivatives markets, which are used by financial speculators as well as producers and commercial users of energy commodities.

The energy futures markets, which date from the 1980s, involve two kinds of traders. Hedgers — producers or commercial users of commodities — trade in futures to offset price risk. They can use the markets to lock in today's price for transactions that will occur in the future, shielding their businesses from unfavorable price changes.[1] Most trading, however, is done by speculators seeking to profit by forecasting price trends. Together, the trading decisions of hedgers and speculators determine commodity prices: there is no better mechanism available for determining prices that will clear markets and ensure efficient allocation of resources than a competitive market where hedgers and speculators pool information and trade on their expectations of future prices.

Since many transactions in the physical markets take place at prices generated by the futures markets, speculators clearly play a large part in setting energy prices. In theory, this should not drive prices away from the fundamental levels: if they trade on faulty assumptions about supply and demand, other traders with superior information — including those who deal in the physical commodities — should be able to profit at their expense. In other words, there is no reason why speculation in and of itself should cause prices to be artificially high.

Theory says increased speculation should produce more efficient pricing. In practice, some observers, including oil company CEOs, OPEC ministers, and investment bank analysts, now speak of a "speculative premium" in the price of oil. This view implies that without speculation, prices could fall significantly without disrupting current patterns of consumption and production. How could the price discovery function of the energy derivatives market have broken?

Several explanations are possible. First, the market could be manipulated. Price manipulation, which is illegal under the Commodity Exchange Act, involves deliberate strategies by a trader or group of traders to push prices to artificial levels. Since derivatives markets reward correct predictions about future prices, manipulation can be very profitable. Most manipulations in the past have involved short-lived price spikes, brought about by spreading false information, or concerted buying or selling. Since 2002, the CFTC has brought 40 enforcement cases involving manipulation, but these do not appear to explain the long-term energy price trends observed in recent years.

It is rare, but possible, for a market to be rigged over a longer period of time — examples include the Hunt brothers' attempt to corner the silver market in 1979-1980 and the manipulation of the copper market by Yasuo Hamanaka of Sumitomo in the mid-1990s — when a single trader or group amasses a dominant position in both physical supplies and futures contracts and obtains enough market power to dictate prices. The CFTC has not produced any evidence that such a grand-scale manipulation of energy prices is underway, and has testified repeatedly that prices are being set competitively.

In the absence of manipulation, another explanation for prices above fundamental levels is a speculative bubble. If, as was the case in the dot-com stock boom, a majority of traders become convinced that a "new era" of value has arrived, they may bid up prices sharply in defiance of counter-arguments based on fundamentals. Eventually, prices return to fundamental levels, often with a sudden plunge. This is what many forecast for energy prices, including George Soros, perhaps the best known speculator of the day.[2]

The bubble explanation is the same as the speculative premium argument. If market participants are trading on mistaken ideas about the fundamentals, they may set a price that is above the true price (which is the current market price minus the speculative premium). However, there is no sure method for determining what the true price is; the only observable price is the one the market generates.

Policy options to discourage speculation driven by irrational exuberance are limited.[3] Actions to reduce the amount of speculative trading, such as increasing the margin requirements or restricting access to the markets, may not produce the desired outcome. Higher margins raise trading costs, which should reduce trading volumes, but the final effect on prices is uncertain. Empirical studies have not found a link between higher margins and lower price volatility, or any evidence that would suggest that prices would fall.[4]

Apart from the possibility that traders in general are getting the price wrong, there is an argument that prices have been driven up by a change in the composition of traders. In recent years, institutional investors — like pension funds, endowments, and foundations — have increasingly chosen to allocate part of their portfolios to commodities. This is rational from the point of view of the individual fund — it may increase investment returns and diversify portfolio risks — but when many institutions follow the same strategy at the same time, the effect can be that of a bubble. A number of bills are aimed at reducing the incidence or impact of institutional investment on the energy markets. These, and other proposals to improve the regulation of derivatives markets, are summarized below.

LEGISLATIVE PROPOSALS: CLOSING LOOPHOLES

Legislative approaches to ensuring that commodity prices are not manipulated or distorted by excessive speculation focus on (1) extending regulatory control to previously unregulated markets, (2) ensuring that speculators cannot use foreign futures markets to avoid U.S. regulation, and (3) restraining the ability of institutional investors (and others who do not deal in the physical commodities themselves) to take large positions in commodities. These three areas are known respectively as the "Enron loophole," the "London loophole," and the "swaps loophole."

The Enron Loophole

The "Enron loophole" refers to a range of transactions that occur off the regulated futures exchanges, in an "over-the-counter" (OTC) market where the CFTC has had little regulatory jurisdiction, and from which it does not receive comprehensive information about who is trading, in what volumes, and at what price.

The Commodity Futures Modernization Act (CFMA, P.L. 106-554) created a statutory exemption from CFTC regulation for certain contracts based on "exempt commodities," defined in the legislation as commodities that are neither agricultural nor financial.[5] Two types of energy derivative markets were thereby exempted: (1) bilateral, negotiated transactions between two counterparties that are not executed on a trading facility,[6] and (2) trades done on an "electronic trading facility." The CFMA specified that these markets must not be accessible to small investors; all traders must be "eligible contract participants" (financial institutions, units of government, or businesses or individuals with substantial financial assets) or, in the case of the electronic trading facility exemption, "eligible commercial entities" (eligible contract participants who either deal in the physical commodity or regularly provide risk management services to those who do).

A substantial volume of over-the-counter energy trading makes use of these exemptions. There is a large market in energy swaps, where investment banks like Goldman Sachs and Morgan Stanley offer contracts linked to energy prices. The OTC market in swaps has also evolved towards an exchange model, where contracts are traded rapidly over an electronic network, and may be backed by a clearing house. The best known of these electronic trading facilities is operated by Intercontinental Exchange Inc

(ICE).[7] The ICE over-the-counter market handles a volume of natural gas contracts roughly equal in size to that handled by Nymex, the largest energy futures exchange.

A Government Accountability Office report in October 2007 noted the growth of the OTC market and raised questions about whether the federal regulator had the information it needed to ensure that markets were free of fraud and manipulation.[8] In the same month, the CFTC issued a report recommending legislative action to increase the transparency of energy markets.[9]

In May 2008, with the farm bill (H.R. 2419, P.L. 110-234), Congress passed legislation that generally follows the CFTC's recommendations and potentially brings part of the OTC market under CFTC regulation. The new law affects electronic trading facilities handling contracts in exempt commodities (primarily energy or metals). If the CFTC determines that a contract traded on such a facility plays a significant price discovery role, that is, if the prices it generates are used as reference points for other transactions and markets, the facility will come under CFTC regulation. The market will have to register with the CFTC, and demonstrate its capacity to comply with several core principles. The principles and requirements include maintaining and enforcing rules against manipulation, establishing position limits or accountability levels to prevent excessive speculation, and providing the CFTC with daily reports on large traders' positions.

The provisions of the Farm Bill, however, do not affect the unregulated status of energy contracts that are not entered into on a trading facility, in other words, the swap market in exempt commodities. Thus, the argument is made that the Enron loophole has been only partially closed. A number of bills propose to end the statutory exemption for OTC energy trades altogether, by putting energy commodities on the same regulatory basis as agricultural commodities. Under current law, derivative contracts based on farm commodities may only be traded on a regulated exchange, unless the CFTC issues an exemption.[10] The CFTC is authorized to grant such exemptions on a case-by-case basis, after determining that the contract would not be against the public interest.

The London Loophole

Unlike the Enron loophole, which addresses the distinction between the regulated exchange markets and the unregulated OTC market, the "London loophole" refers to differences in the oversight of regulated markets in different countries. The U.K. counterpart to Nymex, the leading U.S. energy futures market, is ICE Futures Europe, which is regulated in the U.K. by the Financial Services Authority (FSA).

For several years, the U.K. exchange has been offering energy futures contracts in the United States, via electronic terminals. Ordinarily, an exchange offering futures contracts to U.S. investors is required to register with the CFTC as a "designated contract market," and to comply with all applicable laws and regulations. However, in the case of ICE Futures Europe, the CFTC has waived that requirement, by means of a series of no-action letters, on the grounds that the U.K. market is already regulated at home, and that requiring it to register with the CFTC would be duplicative and add little in terms of market or customer protections.[11]

Initially, the U.K. market offered electronic access to U.S. traders to its most popular contract, a futures contract based on the price of Brent Crude oil, produced in the North Sea. After the market was acquired by ICE, however, it introduced a "look-alike" contract that was identical to Nymex's West Texas Intermediate crude oil future. This contract, which could be settled by making or taking delivery of physical crude oil in the United States, now trades in significant volumes — transactions that would presumably take place on the Nymex otherwise.[12]

With concern over high and volatile energy prices, there has been more scrutiny of ICE Futures Europe's activities in the United States. Can traders avoid speculative position limits by trading on ICE, in addition to (or instead of) Nymex? Does the CFTC receive the same information from ICE Futures Europe about large trading positions that could be a source of manipulation or instability (if they were liquidated suddenly)?

A number of bills propose to close the London loophole, either by requiring foreign boards of trades (exchanges) to comply with all U.S. registration and regulatory requirements if they offer contracts that can be settled by physical delivery within the United States, or by making CFTC relief from such requirements and regulation contingent upon a finding that (1) it will receive from the foreign market information that is comparable or identical to what it receives from domestic exchanges and (2) the foreign market is subject to a regulatory regime that is comparable to the CFTC's.

In the case of ICE Futures Europe, the CFTC announced that it had amended the "no-action relief letter" under which ICE Futures Europe is permitted direct access to U.S. customers. The amended letter conditions direct access on ICE Futures Europe's adoption of equivalent U.S. position limits and accountability levels on its West Texas Intermediate crude oil contract, which is linked to the New York Mercantile Exchange crude oil contract.[13] This agreement complements a 2006 memorandum of understanding with the FSA providing for sharing of trading information.[14]

The CFTC's agreement with ICE appears to fulfill the purposes of several of the bills, but only with respect to the London market. The CFTC has issued other noaction letters granting regulatory waivers to foreign markets, including the Dubai Mercantile Exchange (a joint venture with Nymex), permitting it to offer contracts in the United States (to be cleared by Nymex). On July 7, 2008, the CFTC announced that it would modify the no-action letter to the Dubai exchange on terms similar to the agreement with ICE Futures Europe.[15]

The Swaps Loophole

The view that excessive speculation is driving up energy prices is widely held, but controversial. The question of whether current prices are justified by fundamental factors of supply and demand, or whether irrational exuberance has created a bubble in energy prices (similar to what was observed in dot-com stocks in the late 1990s), is beyond the scope of this report. However, testimony presented to Congress has identified a recent trend in financial markets that some argue may be putting upward pressure on prices — decisions by institutional investors, such as pension funds, foundations, or endowments, to allocate a part of their portfolio to commodities.[16]

From the point of view of a fund manager, investment in commodities may be very attractive under current market conditions. Average returns on stocks and bonds have been relatively low for the past few years, and there is little optimism that they will improve in the near term. Commodities, on the other hand have been the "hot sector." While commodity investment is recognized as being highly risky, a risky asset in a large, diversified portfolio does not necessarily increase overall portfolio risk. The risk of a downturn in commodity prices is not generally correlated with risks in stocks or bonds; in some cases, there may be an inverse relationship. For example, if the price of oil drops suddenly, the institution may lose money on its commodity investment, but the price change will be good for its transportation stocks.

Institutional investors may take positions in commodities in a number of ways, but they do not generally trade on the futures exchanges directly. Instead, they use an intermediary, such as a commodity index fund or an OTC swap contract that is structured to match the return of a published index of commodity prices.[17] As a result of this investment strategy, institutional investors in commodities are often called "index traders."

While the decision of an individual pension fund to put 3%-4% of its portfolio in commodities may appear entirely rational, some observers argue that the aggregate impact of institutional index trading has been to overwhelm the commodity markets, because of the disproportion between the amount of money held by pension funds and others and the amounts that have traditionally been traded in the energy futures market. In other words, index investing is seen as excessive speculation. One particular feature of index trading is the focus of several legislative proposals: the "swaps loophole."

The CFTC and the exchanges maintain position limits or accountability levels that apply to speculative traders. Speculators either face a ceiling on the number of contracts they may own, or, if they breach a position accountability level, they must explain to the exchange why they are accumulating such a large position. The purpose of the speculative limits is to prevent manipulation by speculators with very large positions, and to limit the market impact in cases where losses force speculators to liquidate their positions suddenly.

Position limits do not apply to hedgers, those who use the futures markets to offset price risk arising from their dealings in the underlying commodity. Hedgers are allowed to take positions commensurate with their commercial interests. The rationale for exempting them from position limits is that when they have a hedged position, they have no incentive to manipulate the market: any gains in their futures position will be offset by losses in their physical transactions, and vice versa. (They use the futures markets to lock in today's price, meaning that subsequent price changes do not affect them.)

Traditionally, hedgers have been thought of as those who are active in the physical commodity markets — in the energy market, these would be oil producers, refiners, transporters, and industrial users such as airlines and utilities. With the rise of index trading, however, the definition of hedger has broadened. Both the CFTC and Nymex now extend exemptions from speculative position limits to swaps dealers who are using the futures exchanges to hedge price risk arising from a financial contract with an institutional investor.

In other words, a pension fund wishing to invest in commodities may go to a swaps dealer[18] and enter into a contract that will pay returns equal to the percentage increase in an index of commodity prices. In economic terms, this is equivalent to a long position in futures, which will gain value if the underlying commodity price rises. The swap dealer has, in effect, taken the short side of the trade: it will lose money if prices rise.

The swap dealer is exposed to price risk, and may wish to offset that risk by purchasing exchange-traded futures contracts. Because the dealer is using the futures market to hedge the risk of the swap, the exchanges and the CFTC exempt it from position limits, even though it does not deal in the physical commodity. The rationale is the same as for traditional hedgers: since the swap dealer will gain on its futures position whatever it loses on the swap, and vice versa, it has no incentive to manipulate futures prices.

The effect of this "swaps loophole," however, is to let the ultimate customer — the institutional investors who are clearly speculating on commodity prices — to take larger positions than they would be able to do if they traded directly on the futures exchanges, where they might be constrained by speculative position limits. Hence the description of institutional investors' index trading as excessive speculation.

A number of bills propose to constrain the ability of institutional investors to use the swaps loophole. They would limit the definition of "bona fide hedger" to those who deal in the physical commodity or prohibit trading in OTC energy contracts by those who do not deal in the physical commodity.

Other Legislative Approaches

Raising Margins

Three bills (H.R. 2991, S. 3044, and S. 3183) call for the CFTC to raise margins on oil futures. The margin requirement is the minimum amount of money per futures contract that traders must deposit with their brokers. Margin requirements are set by the exchanges, and are intended to cover losses. At the end of each day, the exchange credits or debits every trader's margin account with the amount of gains or losses. Traders whose margin accounts fall below the minimum requirement will be required to post additional margin before the market opens next day, or their positions may be closed out at a loss.

The exchanges tend to raise margins during periods of price volatility, when the probability of large price swings increases the risk of loss. Nymex has raised the initial margin requirement for crude oil futures contracts (each of which represents 1,000 barrels of oil) several times in 2008.[19]

Since everyone in futures markets trades on margin,[20] raising margins means higher trading costs, which should cause some traders to reduce the size of their positions and reduce trading volume overall. However, as noted above, there is no empirical evidence that higher margins dampen price volatility, making the effect on price uncertain.

Increasing CFTC Resources

Several bills (H.R. 6334, H.R. 6349, and S. 3202) call for supplemental appropriations to permit the CFTC to hire 100 new employees to monitor the energy markets.

Emergency Actions

H.R. 6377, passed by the House on June 26, 2008, and S. 3205 direct the CFTC to use its existing powers, including its emergency authority, to curb immediately the role of excessive speculation in energy and to eliminate price distortion, unreasonable or unwarranted price fluctuations, or any unlawful activities that prevent the market from accurately reflecting the forces of supply and demand for energy. (CFTC's emergency authority includes the power to set margin levels or to order the liquidation of trading positions.)

Studies of the Market

A number of bills call for studies of various aspects of the market, including the effects of raising margin, the adequacy of international regulation, the effects of speculation, and the impact of index trading on prices.

Table 1 below provides summaries of all legislation that bears on the regulation of energy speculation.

Table 1. Summaries of Energy Futures and Speculation Bills

Bill Number/ Sponsor	Status	Summary
H.Res. 1278 (Rep. Petri)	Referred to the Committee on Foreign Affairs	Expresses the sense of the House that the United States should lead an international diplomatic initiative to limit inefficient speculation on international energy exchanges through the adoption of international standards for energy futures trading margin requirements as an appropriate means of ensuring access to reliable and affordable supplies of crude oil.
H.Res. 1289 (Rep. Shays)	Referred to the House Committee on Agriculture	Urges the CFTC to require institutional investors to abide by position limits already established for the greater crude oil trading community, and urges the President to direct the CFTC to work with the United Kingdom Financial Services Authority to establish position limits on oil futures traded on the Intercontinental Exchange that are similar to those that apply to traders on the New York Mercantile Exchange.

Table 1. (Continued)

Bill Number/ Sponsor	Status	Summary
H.R. 594 (Rep. Stupak)	Referred to House Subcommittee on General Farm Commodities and Risk Management	Prevent Unfair Manipulation of Prices Act of 2007. Creates a new regulatory category, "included energy transactions," encompassing over-the-counter transactions in energy derivatives that play a significant role in determining prices paid in the cash market for the underlying commodities. Sets for-th reporting and record-keeping requirements for included energy transactions, requiring that certain information about price and trading volumes (as well as other information the CFTC needs to prevent and detect price manipulation) be made available to regulators and/or the public. Clarifies prohibitions against commodity fraud and manipulation, and increases civil and criminal penalties for violations.
H.R. 2419 (Rep. Peterson)	P.L. 110-234 enacted May 22, 2008, over the President's veto	Food Conservation and Energy Act of 2008 (the Farm Bill). Title XIII included provisions reauthorizing the CFTC and creates a new regulatory regime for certain OTC energy derivatives markets, subjecting them to a number of exchange-like regulations. The provisions apply to "electronic trading facilities" — markets where multiple buyers and sellers are able to post orders and execute transactions over an electro-nic network. If the CFTC determines that a contract traded on these markets, previously exempt from most regulation, plays a significant role in setting the price of the underlying commodity, they will be required to register with the CFTC and comply with several regulatory core principles aimed at curbing manipulation and excessive speculation (including the establishment and enforcement of position limits). They will be required to publish and/or report to the CFTC information relating to prices, trading volume, and size of positions held by speculators and hedgers. These new regulatory requirements apply only to electronic markets that have come to resemble the regulated futures exchanges. Bilateral OTC derivative contracts between two principals (e.g., between a swap dealer and an institutional investor), that are not executed on a trading facility where multiple bids and offers are displayed, will continue to be largely exempt from CFTC regulation.
H.R. 3009 (Rep. Barrow)	Referred to House Subcommittee on General Farm Commodities and Risk Management	Market Transparency Reporting of United States Transac-tions Act of 2007. Imposes reporting requirements on OTC contracts in natural gas. The information to be disclosed shall be sufficient to enable the CFTC to assess the overall trading activities, potential market power, and concentration of positions held by the largest traders. The CFTC shall publish a report setting out the information received, in aggregate form.
H.R. 4066 (Rep. Welch)	Referred to House Committee	Close the Enron Loophole Act. Defines a new regulated entity — "energy trading facility" — an OTC market that plays a significant role in price discovery. Requires energy

	on Agriculture	trading facilities (ETFs) to register with the CFTC, and sets out criteria for registration, including the capacity to monitor trading to prevent manipulation and excessive speculation. ETFs must also establish and enforce speculative position limits that are comparable to the limits that apply to regulated futures exchanges, and must publish data on trading volumes and prices. Also imposes reporting and recordkeeping requirements on transactions on foreign futures exchanges that involve delivery of energy commodities within the United States, where such transactions are executed on terminals located in the U.S.
H.R. 6130 (Rep. Barton)	Referred to the Committee on Agriculture, and in addition to the Committee on Energy and Commerce	Calls for an interagency study of the effects of speculation in the futures markets (including foreign futures markets) for natural gas, crude oil, and gasoline on cash market and retail prices for the commodities. Directs the CFTC to issue a regulation setting out how it determines whether futures and derivatives regulation in a foreign country is comparable to U.S. regulation of those markets.
H.R. 6238 (Rep. Dingell)	Referred to the House Committee on Energy and Commerce	Directs the Secretary of Energy to establish an interagency working group to study the impact of market speculation and manipulation on the price of crude oil and refined petro-leum products and the international regulation of trading markets. The working group shall issue a report within one year, and shall make recommendations for legislative or regulatory action at any time if needed to protect U.S. ener-gy consumers from the potential for abuse and manipulation by activities taking place in energy markets or exchanges.
H.R. 6264 (Rep. Larson)	Referred to the House Committee on Agriculture	Limits over-the-counter derivative transactions in energy commodities (defined as crude oil, heating oil, gasoline, or diesel fuel) to persons whom the CFTC has certified as having the capacity to produce, manufacture, or accept physical delivery of the commodity.
H.R. 6279 (Rep. Chabot)	Referred to the House Committee on Agriculture	Oil Speculation Reduction Act of 2008. Prohibits the CFTC from exempting from U.S. regulation a foreign board of trade that offers contracts in crude oil to be physically delivered in the United States, unless (1) the foreign market applies principles or requirements daily publication of trading information and position limits or accountability levels for speculators that are comparable to those applied by U.S. exchanges, (2) provides the CFTC with information about large trading positions compare-able to what the CFTC receives from U.S. markets, and (3) imposes margin requirements that are comparable to those in U.S. markets and sufficient to reduce excessive speculation and protect consumers. CFTC shall, within 18 months of enactment, review waivers of regulation already extended to foreign exchanges, and shall report to Congress within 12 months on the implemen-tation of this act.

Table 1. (Continued)

Bill Number/ Sponsor	Status	Summary
H.R. 6284 (Rep. Matheson)	Referred to the House Committee on Agriculture	Authorizes the CFTC to apply anti-manipulation and certain other provisions of the Commodity Exchange Act to persons located in the United States trading on foreign futures exchanges, and to require such person to limit, reduce, or liquidate any position to prevent or reduce the threat of price manipulation, excessive speculation, price distortion, or disruption of delivery or the cash settlement process. Limits the CFTC's authority to exempt foreign futures markets that offer contracts based on "an energy commodity that is physically delivered in the United States" from U.S. regulation. Before granting such relief from regulation, CFTC must determine that the foreign market applies principles regarding the publication of trading in-formation and position limits or accountability levels for speculators that are comparable to U.S. law and regula-tion, and that the CFTC receives from the foreign market the same information regarding large trader positions that it receives from U.S. exchanges. Requires the CFTC to reevaluate within 18 months any foreign markets to which it has previously granted relief from U.S. registration requirements.
H.R. 6330 (Rep. Stupak)	Referred to the Committee on Agriculture, and to the Committee on Energy and Commerce	Prevent Unfair Manipulation of Prices Act of 2008. Specifies that "energy commodities" (as defined) are not exempt commodities. As a result, trading in OTC contracts in energy commodities would not be exempted from regulation by statute, but would require CFTC approval on a case-by-case basis, which could be granted only after 60-day notification to Congress and a public comment period. Bilateral OTC energy contracts (not executed on a trading facility) would be subject to reporting and recordkeeping requirements. Foreign futures markets offering contracts in the United States, with a delivery point in the United States, would be subject to U.S. regulation. The definition of "bona fide hedger" would exclude those hedging price risk arising from energy swaps. The CFTC would be required to publish certain information about trading strategies that track commodity price indexes, including the size of positions and the total value of index speculation. Provides FERC with cease-and-desist authority to freeze the assets of companies prosecuted under its antimanipulation authority.
H.R. 6334 (Rep. Etheridge)	Referred to the House Committee on Agriculture	Expresses the sense of the House that the President should request emergency appropriations for the CFTC in FY2008, in order to hire 100 additional employees to monitor and improve enforcement in energy markets. Directs the CFTC, before granting relief from U.S. registration and regulatory requirements to any foreign market offering contracts involving delivery of energy commodities in the United States, to determine that the foreign market applies regulations regarding publication of trading data and position limits that are comparable to U.S. regulations, and that the foreign market supplies the CFTC with the same

		type of information about large speculative and hedging positions that the CFTC now obtains from U.S. exchanges. Directs the CFTC to publish monthly data on the positions of index funds (and other passive, longonly positions) in energy markets, including the total amount of such investments and the size of speculative positions compared to those of hedgers who deal in the physical commodities.
H.R. 6341 (Rep. Van Hollen)	Referred to the House Committee on Agriculture	Energy Markets Anti-Manipulation and Integrity Restoration Act . Removes "energy commodities" (as defined) from the category of exempt commodities, thus ending the statutory exemption from CFTC regulation for OTC energy contracts. Specifies that a board of trade, exchange, or market shall not be considered to be foreign if it has a trading affiliate or trading infrastructure located in the United States; and a contract of sale of an energy commodity for future delivery in the United States, which is a significant price discovery contract (as determined by the CFTC) for the energy commodity, is executed or traded on or through the board of trade, exchange, or market.
H.R. 6349 (Rep. J. Marshall)	Referred to the House Committee on Agriculture	Increasing Transparency and Accountability in Oil Prices Act of 2008. Expresses the sense of the House that the President should request emergency appropriations for the CFTC, to fund 100 new positions to oversee energy futures market speculation and help restore public confidence. Establishes the Office of Inspector General as an independent office within the CFTC. Calls for a GAO study of international regulation of energy derivatives. Limits the CFTC's authority to exempt foreign futures markets that offer contracts based on "an energy commodity that is physically delivered in the United States" from U.S. regulation. Before granting such relief from regulation, CFTC must determine that the foreign market applies principles regarding the publication of trading information and
		position limits or accountability levels for speculators that are comparable to U.S. law and regulation, and that the CFTC receives from the foreign market the same information regarding large trader positions that it receives from U.S. exchanges. Requires the CFTC to reevaluate within 18 months any foreign markets to which it has previously granted relief from U.S. registration requirements. Expands CFTC jurisdiction over certain trades by U.S. persons executed on foreign markets. Directs the CFTC to require detailed reporting from swaps dealers and index traders, and to review index trading to ensure that it does not adversely impact the price discovery process. Requires the CFTC to publish monthly data on the number and total of index funds and data on speculative positions relative to bona fide physical hedger positions.

Table 1. (Continued)

Bill Number/ Sponsor	Status	Summary
H.R. 6372 (Rep. Hill)	Referred to the House Committee on Agriculture	Commodity Futures Restoration Act. Removes energy commodities (as defined) from the class of exempt commodities. Puts energy swaps on the same regulatory basis as agricultural commodity swaps. A futures exchange shall not be considered foreign if (1) it has an affiliate located in the United States, (2) it trades a contract settled by delivery in the United States, or (3) it trades a significant price discovery contract. Exemptions from position limits for bona fide hedgers shall not apply to swaps involving energy commodities. Directs the CFTC to report to Congress within 90 days of enactment on margin levels and position limits applicable to energy commodities.
H.R. 6377 (Rep. Peterson)	Passed the House, June 26, 2008	Energy Markets Emergency Act of 2008. Directs the CFTC to utilize all its authority, including its emergency powers, to: (1) curb immediately the role of excessive speculation in any contract market within the jurisdiction and control of the Commodity Futures Trading Commission, on or through which energy futures or swaps are traded; and (2) eliminate excessive speculation, price distortion, sudden or unreasonable fluctuations or unwarranted changes in prices, or other unlawful activity that is causing major market disturbances that prevent the market from accurately reflecting the forces of supply and demand for energy commodities.
S. 577 (Sen. Feinstein)	Referred to the Senate Committee on Agriculture, Nutrition, and Forestry	Oil and Gas Traders Oversight Act of 2007. Amends the Commodity Exchange Act to prescribe reporting and recordkeeping requirements for positions involving energy commodities (a commodity or the derivatives of a commodity used primarily as a source of energy). Directs the Commodity Futures Trading Commission to subject to the requirements of this Act a contract, agreement, or transaction for future delivery in an energy commodity.
S. 2058 (Sen. Levin)	Referred to the Senate Committee on Agriculture, Nutrition, and Forestry	Close the Enron Loophole Act. Defines a new regulated entity — "energy trading facility" — an OTC market that plays a significant role in price discovery. Requires energy trading facilities (ETFs) to register with the CFTC, and sets out criteria for registration, including the capacity to monitor trading to prevent manipulation and excessive speculation. ETFs must also establish and enforce speculative position limits that are comparable to the limits that apply to regulated futures exchanges, and must publish data on trading volumes and prices. Also imposes reporting and recordkeeping requirements on transactions on foreign futures exchanges that involve delivery of energy commodities within the United States, where such transactions are executed on terminals located in the U.S.
S. 2991 (Sen.	Placed on	Consumer-First Energy Act of 2008 - Sec. 501 limits the

Reid)	Senate Legislative Calendar under General Orders	CFTC's authority to exempt foreign futures markets that offer contracts based on "an energy commodity that is physically delivered in the United States" from U.S. regulation. Before granting such relief from regulation, CFTC must determine that the foreign market applies principles regarding the publication of trading information and position limits or accountability levels for speculators that are compar-able to U.S. law and regulation, and that the CFTC receives from the foreign market the same informat-ion regarding large trader positions that it receives from U.S. exchanges. Requires the CFTC to reevaluate any foreign markets to which it has previously granted relief from U.S. registration requirements. Sec. 502 directs the CFTC to issue within 90 days of enactment regulations setting " a substantial increase in margin levels for crude oil traded on any trading facility" under CFTC's jurisdiction. Calls for CFTC and GAO to conduct separate studies on the impact of increases in margin requirements.
S. 2995 (Sen. Levin)	Referred to the Committee on Agriculture, Nutrition, and Forestry	Oil Trading Transparency Act. Limits the CFTC's authority to exempt foreign futures markets that offer contracts based on "an energy commodity that is physically delivered in the United States" from U.S. regulation. Before granting such relief from regulation, CFTC must determine that the foreign market applies principles regarding position limits or accountability levels for speculators and publication of trading information that are compare-able to U.S. law and regu-lation, and that the CFTC receives from the foreign market the same information regarding large trader positions that it receives from U.S. exchanges. Requires the CFTC to reevaluate any foreign markets to which it has previously granted relief from U.S. registration requirements.
S. 3044 (Sen. Reid)	Motion to pro-ceed to meas-ure considered in Senate	Consumer-First Energy Act of 2008. Includes provisions related to foreign futures markets and an increase in oil futures margins identical to S. 2991.
S. 3081 (Sen. Kerry)	Referred to the Committee on the Judiciary	Establishes a Petroleum Industry Antitrust Task Force within the Department of Justice to examine, among other issues, the existence and effects of any anticompetitive manipulation in futures markets or other trading exchanges relating to petroleum or petroleum products.
S. 3122 (Sen.Cantwell)	Referred to the Senate Committee on Agriculture, Nutrition, and Forestry	Policing United States Oil Commodities Markets Act of 2008. Requires foreign markets "that operate trading termi-nals in the United States, on which are traded contracts that serve a price discovery function for any energy commodity that is delivered in the United States" to register with the CFTC as designated contract markets (or regulated exchan-ges). Also applies to markets to which CFTC has already granted relief from registration requirements.

Table 1. (Continued)

Bill Number/ Sponsor	Status	Summary
S. 3129 (Sen. Levin et al.)	Referred to the Committee on Agriculture, Nutrition, and Forestry	Close the London Loophole Act of 2008. Authorizes the CFTC to apply anti-manipulation and certain other provisions of the Commodity Exchange Act to persons located in the United States trading on foreign futures exchanges, and to require such person to limit, reduce, or liquidate any position to prevent or reduce the threat of price manipulation, excessive speculation, price distortion, or disruption of delivery or the cash settlement process. Limits the CFTC's authority to exempt foreign futures markets that offer contracts based on "an energy commodity that is physically delivered in the United States" from U.S. regulation. Before granting such relief from regulation, CFTC must determine that the foreign market applies principles regarding the publication of trading information and position limits or accountability levels for speculators that are comparable to U.S. law and regulation, and that the CFTC receives from the foreign market the same information regarding large trader positions that it receives from U.S. exchanges. Requires the CFTC to reevaluate within 18 months any foreign markets to which it has previously gran-ted relief from U.S. registration requirements.
S. 3130 (Sen. Durbin)	Referred to the Committee on Agriculture, Nutrition, and Forestry	Increasing Transparency and Accountability in Oil Prices Act. Expresses the sense of the Senate favoring a supplemental appropriation to increase the CFTC's resources, including the hiring of 100 new employees to monitor energy futures markets. Establishes the Office of Inspector general as an independent office within the CFTC. Directs GAO to study the international regime for regulating the trading of energy commodity futures and derivatives. Includes provisions related to foreign futures markets identical to S. 2991.
S. 3131 (Sens. Feinstein and Stevens)	Referred to the Senate Committee on Agriculture, Nutrition, and Forestry	Oil Speculation Control Act of 2008. Makes institutional investors who trade in energy contracts but do not take or make physical delivery of energy commodities subject to speculative position limits or accountability levels. Defines "bona fide hedging transactions" as those related to price risk arising from physical energy transactions.
		Establishes the Office of Inspector general as an independent office within the CFTC. Extends large trader reporting requirements to index traders, swap dealers, and institutional investors. Directs the CFTC to review the trading practices of index traders, swap dealers, and institutional investors in markets under CFTC jurisdiction to ensure that such practices are not impeding the price discovery process, to gather information, and to assess the adequacy of current regulation of such trading practices. Directs the CFTC to use its emergency authority to impose a 60-day freeze to prevent institutional investors from increasing the size of their positions in energy commodity

		futures or commodity future index funds.
S. 3134 (Sen. B. Nelson)	Referred to the Committee on Agriculture, Nutrition, and Forestry	Removes energy commodities (as defined) from the class of exempt commodities. Transactions in energy commodities will be subject to the same degree of regulation under the Commodity Exchange Act as agricultural commodities. That is, there will no longer be a statutory exemption for OTC energy trades.
S. 3183 (Sen. Dorgan)	Referred to the Committee on Agriculture, Nutrition, and Forestry	Directs the CFTC to use its authority to eliminate manipula-tion and speculation from the petroleum futures market. Requires the CFTC to distinguish between "legitimate hedge trading" — transactions involving comercial producers and consumers of physical petroleum products — and all other trades. Requires the CFTC to revoke or modify all prior actions or decisions, (including exemptions from position limits for trading other than legitimate hedge trading) that prevent the CFTC from protecting legitimate hedge trades and discouraging speculative trades. Requires the CFTC to order an increase in petroleum futures margin requirements to at least 25% for trades not classified as legitimate hedge trading. Requires the CFTC to convene an international working group of regulators to ensure the protection of petroleum futures market from excessive speculation and world wide forum shopping.
S. 3185 (Sen. Cantwell)	Referred to the Committee on Agriculture, Nutrition, and Forestry	Identical to H.R. 6330.
S. 3202 (Sen. McConnell)	Placed on Senate Legislative Calendar under General Orders. Calendar No. 854	Gas Price Reduction Act of 2008. (Title IV — Energy Commodity Markets.) Directs the President's Working Group on Financial Markets to study the international regu-lation of energy derivatives. Bars the CFTC from permitting direct access by U.S. invest-tors to foreign futures markets trading contracts that settle on prices of U.S. contracts, unless those markets (1) publish trading data comparable to U.S. futures exchanges, (2) ado-
		pt position limits comparable to U.S. limits, and (3) provide the CFTC with large trader re-ports comparable to what the CFTC receives from U.S. markets. Directs the CFTC to set reporting requirements for swap dealers and index traders, and to publish monthly aggregate figures on index investing and other passive, long-only strategies in energy and agricultural commodities. Directs the CFTC to hire 100 new employees for monitoring and enforcement in energy markets, and authorizes appropriations for this purpose.

Table 1. (Continued)

Bill Number/ Sponsor	Status	Summary
S. 3205 (Sen. Cantwell)	Referred to the Committee on Agriculture, Nutrition, and Forestry	A bill to direct the Commodity Futures Trading Commi-ssion to utilize all its authority, including its emergency powers, to curb immediately the role of excessive specula-tion in any contract market within the jurisdiction and con-trol of the Commodity Futures Trading Commission, on or through which energy futures or swaps are traded, and to eliminate excessive speculation, price distortion, sudden or unreasonable fluctuations or unwarranted changes in prices, or other unlawful activity that is causing major market dis-turbances that prevent the market from accurately reflecting the forces of supply and demand for energy commodities.

APPENDIX: MECHANICS OF FUTURES CONTRACTS

The Mechanics of a Futures Contract

An oil futures contract represents 1,000 barrels of oil, but neither party to the contract need ever possess the actual commodity. (Contracts may be settled by physical delivery, but in practice the vast majority are settled in cash.) When a contract is made today, one party (called the "long") agrees to buy oil at a future date from the other (the "short"). Contracts are available with different maturities, designated by expiration months, but the size is always the same. (In oil, there is a contract expiring every month.) The price at which this future transaction is to take place is the current market price. Assuming the price of oil is $135 per barrel, the long trader is committed to buy at that price, and the short is obliged to sell.

Assume that tomorrow the price of oil goes to $140/barrel. The long trader now has the advantage: he is entitled to buy for $135 oil that is now worth $140. His profit is $5,000 (the $5 per barrel increase times the 1,000 barrels specified in the contract). The short has lost the identical amount: she is obliged to sell oil for less than the going price.

If, on the following day, the price goes to $145, the long gains another $5,000. The short, down a total of $10,000, may reconsider her investment strategy and decide to exit the market. She can do this at any time by entering into an offsetting, or opposite transaction. That is, she purchases a long contract with the same expiration date. Her obligation (on paper) is now to sell 1,000 barrels (according to the first contract) and to buy 1,000 barrels (the second contract) when both contracts expire simultaneously. Whatever price prevails at that time, the net effect of the two transaction will be zero. The short's position is said to be "evened out" — she is out of the market.

The short's decision to exit does not affect the long, who may prefer to ride with the trend. This is because all contracts are assumed by the exchange's clearing house, which becomes the opposite party on each trade, and guarantees payment. The ability to enter and exit the market by offset, without having to make or take delivery of the physical commodity, permits trading strategies based on short-term price expectations. While some traders may keep a long or short position open for weeks or months, others buy and sell within a time frame of minutes or seconds.

The exchange clearing house, which guarantees all trades, also controls traders' funds. Before entering into the trade described above, both long and short would have been required to deposit an initial margin payment of $11,813. (The amount is set by the exchange; the figure is current as of June 30, 2008.) All contracts are priced, or "marked-to-market," each day. The long trader above would have had his $10,000 gain credited to his margin account, while the short would have had to make additional "maintenance" margin payments to cover her losses. It is worth noting that her two-day $10,000 loss represents 85% of her original investment, that is, her initial margin deposit of $11,813: the risks of futures speculation are high. When traders exit the market, any funds remaining in their margin accounts are returned. (Other transaction costs, such as brokerage commissions and exchange fees, are not returnable.)

Options on futures are also available for many futures contracts. The holder of an option has the right (but not the obligation) to enter into a long or short futures contract over the life of the option. The option will only be exercised if price movements are favorable to the option buyer, that is, if the underlying futures contract would be profitable. The seller of the option receives a payment (called a premium) for granting this right. The seller profits if the option is not exercised by the buyer.

End Notes

[1] See the Appendix for a description of the mechanics of a futures contract.
[2] Soros, however, argues that an energy "bust" may be forestalled by new regulation on commodity index speculation by institutional investors. Testimony of George Soros before the Senate Commerce Committee, June 3, 2008, available at [http://commerce.senate.gov/public/_files/SorosFinalTestimony.pdf].
[3] See CRS Report RL33666, *Asset Bubbles: Economic Effects and Policy Options for the Federal Reserve*, by Marc Labonte.

[4] Some argue, in fact, that higher margins might actually drive prices higher, since many long speculative positions are held by large institutional investors who would have no trouble meeting any margin demand.

[5] See CRS Report RS21401, *Regulation of Energy Derivatives*, by Mark Jickling, for information on the CFMA.

[6] The term "trading facility" is defined in the Commodity Exchange Act as a person or group of persons that constitutes, maintains, or provides a physical or electronic facility or system in which multiple participants have the ability to execute or trade agreements, contracts, or transactions by accepting bids and offers made by other participants that are open to multiple participants in the facility or system.

[7] ICE is a publicly traded firm, based in Atlanta, that also owns the largest regulated energy futures market in Europe, ICE Futures Europe (formerly the International Petroleum Exchange, located in London).

[8] U.S. Government Accountability Office, *Trends in Energy Derivatives Markets Raise Questions about CFTC's Oversight*, GAO 08-25, October 2007, 83 p.

[9] U.S. Commodity Futures Trading Commission, *Report on the Oversight of Trading on Regulated Futures Exchanges and Exempt Commercial Markets*, October 2007, 23 p.

[10] Exemptive authority is provided by section 4(c) of the Commodity Exchange Act.

[11] The first no-action letter was issued in 1999, when the market was known as the International Petroleum Exchange. When the IPE was acquired by ICE (a U.S. firm), in 2001, the waiver continued, and was modified several times.

[12] In 2007, Nymex traded 121.5 million WTI futures contracts, while ICE Futures Europe traded 51.4 million. "Volume Surges Again," *Futures Industry Magazine*, March/April 2008, p. 23.

[13] U.S. Commodity Futures Trading Commission, "CFTC Conditions Foreign Access on Adoption of Position Limits on London Crude Oil Contract," Release 5511-08, June 17, 2008.

[14] Online at [http://www.cftc.gov/newsroom/generalpressreleases/2006/pr5259-06.html].

[15] U.S. Commodity Futures Trading Commission, "CFTC Grants Relief to NYMEX in Connection with Clearing Contracts Traded on the Dubai Mercantile Exchange DME Trading System to be Available in U.S.," Release 5339-07, May 25, 2007; and "CFTC Grants Exemption to NYMEX in Connection with Three New Contracts to be Traded on the Dubai Mercantile Exchange," Release 5495-08, May 1, 2008.

[16] Testimony of Michael W. Masters before the Senate Committee on Homeland Security and Governmental Affairs, May 20, 2008, available at [http://hsgac.senate.gov/public/_files/052008Masters.pdf].

[17] Examples of such indices are the Dow Jones-AIG Commodity Index, or the Goldman Sachs Commodity Index, which are variously weighted among farm products, energy commodities, and metals. A swap contract is a derivative economically equivalent to a futures contract: two parties agree to exchange payments over the life of a contract that are linked to a price, index, or other variable. Depending on which way the underlying variable moves, the cash flows will be net positive for one counterparty, and negative for the other.

[18] The major swap dealers in energy markets are investment banks like Goldman Sachs and Morgan Stanley.

[19] At the beginning of 2008, the crude oil margin requirement was $6,075; on July 1, 2008, it was raised to $12,488. (Both figures are for customers; margin requirements for exchange members are slightly lower.)

[20] This is unlike the stock market, where margin refers to loans extended to buy stock (and collateralized by the purchased securities). Relatively few stock purchases are made on margin.

In: Energy Prices: Supply, Demand …   ISBN: 978-1-60741-374-5
Editor: John T. Perry   © 2010 Nova Science Publishers, Inc.

Chapter 2

COMMODITY FUTURES TRADING COMMISSION: REPORT TO CONGRESSIONAL ADDRESSEES

Government Accountability Office

Why GAO Did This Study

Prices for four energy commodities—crude oil, heating oil, unleaded gasoline, and natural gas—have risen substantially since 2002. Some observers believe that higher energy prices are the result of changes in supply and demand. Others believe that increased futures trading activity has also contributed to higher prices. This report, conducted under the Comptroller General of the United States' authority, examines trends and patterns in the physical and energy derivatives markets, (2) the scope of the Commodity Futures Trading Commission's (CFTC) regulatory authority over these markets, and (3) the effectiveness of CFTC's monitoring and detection of market abuses and enforcement. For this work, GAO analyzed futures and large trader data and interviewed market participants, experts, and officials at six federal agencies.

What GAO Recommends

As part of CFTC's reauthorization process, Congress should consider further exploring the scope of the agency's authority over energy derivatives trading, in particular for trading in exempt commercial markets. In addition, GAO recommends that CFTC improve the usefulness of the information provided to the public, better document its monitoring activities, and develop more outcome-oriented performance measures for its enforcement program. In written comments, CFTC generally agreed with GAO's recommendations.

What GAO Found

Rising energy prices have been attributed to a variety of factors, among them recent trends (2002-2006) in the physical and futures markets. These trends include (1) factors in the physical markets, such as tight supply, rising demand, and a lack of spare production capacity; (2) higher than average, but declining, volatility (a measure of the degree to which prices fluctuate over time) in energy futures prices for crude oil, heating oil, and unleaded gasoline; and (3) growth in several key areas, including the number of noncommercial participants in the futures markets (including hedge funds), the volume of energy futures contracts traded, and the volume of energy derivatives traded outside of traditional futures exchanges. Because these changes took place concurrently, the effect of any individual trend or factor is unclear.

On the basis of its authority under the Commodity Exchange Act (CEA), CFTC focuses its oversight primarily on the operations of traditional futures exchanges, such as the New York Mercantile Exchange, Inc. (NYMEX), where energy futures are traded. Energy derivatives are also traded on other markets, namely, exempt commercial and over-the-counter (OTC) markets, that are exempt from CFTC oversight. Both types of markets have seen their volumes climb in recent years. Exempt commercial markets are electronic trading facilities where certain commodities, such as energy, are traded between large, sophisticated participants. OTC markets allow eligible parties to enter into contracts directly, without using an exchange. While the exempt commercial and OTC markets are subject to the CEA's antimanipulation and antifraud provisions and CFTC enforcement of those provisions, some market observers question whether CFTC needs broader authority to oversee these markets. CFTC is currently examining the effects of trading in the regulated and exempt energy markets on price discovery and the scope of its authority over these markets—an issue that will warrant further examination as part of the CFTC reauthorization process. Moreover, because of changes and innovations in the market, the methods used to categorize these data can distort the information reported to the public, which may not be completely accurate or relevant.

CFTC conducts daily surveillance of trading on NYMEX that is designed to detect and deter fraudulent or abusive trading practices involving energy futures contracts. To detect abusive practices, such as potential manipulation, CFTC uses various information sources and relies heavily on trading activity data for large market participants. Using this information, CFTC staff may pursue alleged abuse or manipulation. However, because the agency does not maintain complete records of all such allegations, this lack of information makes it difficult to determine the usefulness and extent of these activities. In addition, CFTC's performance measures for enforcement do not fully reflect the program's goals and purposes, which could be addressed by developing additional outcome-based performance measures that more fully reflect progress in meeting the program's overall goals.

October 19, 2007

Congressional Addressees

The price of energy commodities—crude oil, unleaded gasoline, heating oil, and natural gas—increased significantly from 2002 to 2006, negatively affecting consumers and the U.S. economy. While increased energy prices generally are attributed to normal market forces of supply and demand, some observers have questioned whether trading activity in energy futures contracts and other types of energy derivatives placed upward pressure on prices during this period.[1] A futures contract is an agreement to purchase or sell a commodity for delivery in the future.[2] Like other types of derivatives, its price is based on the value of an underlying commodity, such as natural gas or oil. While futures prices are determined on the basis of prices in the market where physical goods and commodities are sold (physical market), buyers and sellers of natural gas, crude oil, gasoline, and other energy products are influenced by the futures prices of these commodities when determining their prices. Trading in futures contracts has grown significantly since 2001, in part because of trading by new market participants, such as hedge funds, and increased investment in commodity index funds.[3]

The surge in energy prices and the growth in the volume of futures contracts and other derivatives have renewed questions about the adequacy of the Commodity Futures Trading Commission's (CFTC) authority and ability to oversee derivatives that are traded off exchange, or over the counter (OTC). CFTC's primary mission includes preserving the integrity of the futures markets and protecting market users and the public from fraud, manipulation, and abusive trading practices.[4] In 2000, CFTC's authority regarding futures contracts and other types of derivatives was clarified by the Commodity Futures Modernization Act of 2000 (CFMA). Among other things, the CFMA specifically authorizes off-exchange derivatives trading by establishing a framework that tailors the level of regulation of a market to the products being traded and the market's participants. Under the act, some exchanges (e.g., the New York Mercantile Exchange, Inc. (NYMEX)), that allow all types of traders, including retail customers, to access their facilities are regulated, while other venues that are off exchange can be accessed only by large, sophisticated traders and are either largely unregulated or exempt from regulation. Like futures markets, these unregulated, off-exchange markets also have grown significantly, raising questions about the amount of regulatory scrutiny that CFTC should provide.

This report, conducted under the Comptroller General of the United States' authority, addresses concerns raised by Congress, consumer groups, states' attorneys general, and others about rising prices in energy markets and the relationship, if any, of futures trading to rising energy prices. We addressed this report to you because of your expressed interest or your committee's jurisdiction. This report focuses on four energy commodities— crude oil, unleaded gasoline, natural gas, and heating oil—and CFTC's oversight of these commodities. Specifically, this report examines (1) trends and patterns of trading activity in the physical and energy derivatives markets and the effects of those trends on prices; (2) the scope of CFTC's authority for protecting market users from fraudulent, manipulative, and abusive practices in the trading of energy futures contracts; and (3) the effectiveness of CFTC's monitoring and detection of market abuses in energy futures markets and in connection with energy-related enforcement actions.

To address these objectives, we obtained and analyzed end-of-the-day trading data for energy futures contracts from NYMEX and data from CFTC's large trader reporting system (LTRS) database, which we tested and found reliable for our purposes.[5] We obtained and analyzed other CFTC records and reports relevant to the commission's surveillance and other activities. We also reviewed applicable laws, regulations, and policy statements. We obtained information from a broad range of participants in the energy futures markets and officials knowledgeable about the futures markets. These individuals included officials from large oil companies, refiners, trade associations representing end users of natural gas, investment banks, and hedge funds as well as energy consultants and academic experts. We interviewed officials in CFTC's Division of Market Oversight, Division of Enforcement, Office of the Chief Economist, Office of the General Counsel, and Office of the Inspector General. Moreover, because CFTC oversight is also provided through officials located in the commission's field offices, we obtained information from officials at the CFTC New York Regional Office, which conducts surveillance of futures trading on NYMEX. In addition, we gathered and analyzed information on oversight of the energy markets provided by other federal agencies, including the U.S. Department of Energy's Energy Information Administration (EIA), the Federal Energy Regulatory Commission (FERC), the Federal Trade Commission (FTC), the Department of Justice (DOJ), and the Securities and Exchange Commission (SEC). We conducted our work in Chicago, Houston, New York City, and Washington, D.C., between July 2005 and September 2007 in accordance with generally accepted government auditing standards. Appendix I contains a more detailed description of our scope and methodology.

RESULTS IN BRIEF

Significant changes occurred in both physical and energy derivatives markets between 2002 and 2006 that were accompanied by rising energy prices; however, it is difficult to precisely determine the extent or effect of any single factor on energy prices. Specifically:

- There was a tight supply and rising demand in the physical markets for crude oil, heating oil, unleaded gasoline, and natural gas, stemming from various factors—such as increased political instability in some of the major oil-producing countries, decreased spare oil production capacity, refining capacity that did not expand at the same pace as demand for gasoline, and rapidly rising global demand for energy products.
- Volatility (a measure of the degree to which prices fluctuate over time) in energy futures prices generally remained above historic

averages in 2002 and 2003, but declined through 2006 for crude oil, heating oil, and unleaded gasoline.
- The number of noncommercial participants in the futures markets, the volume of energy futures contracts traded, and the volume of energy derivatives traded outside traditional futures exchange also have grown steadily.

Reasonable arguments have been made that events in physical and futures markets contributed in some degree to the increases in inflation-adjusted energy prices in both markets during this period for crude oil, unleaded gasoline, and heating oil. However, opinions vary on how much the recent changes in the financial markets influenced energy prices. For example, some market participants and observers have argued that speculation alone could not have influenced prices artificially over such a long period, while others have concluded that increased trading activity put upward pressure on the prices of spot as well as futures contracts.

Under the Commodity Exchange Act (CEA), CFTC's authority for protecting market users from fraudulent, manipulative, and abusive practices in energy derivatives trading is primarily focused on the operations of traditional futures exchanges, such as NYMEX, where energy futures are traded. To help provide transparency to the public, CFTC publishes aggregate trading information for large commercial (such as oil companies and refineries) and noncommercial (such as hedge funds) traders for various commodities through its Commitment of Traders (COT) reports. These reports include the number of traders, changes since the last report, and open positions—an obligation to take or make delivery of a commodity in the future without a matching obligation in the opposite direction. However, because of changes and innovation in the market, methods used to categorize these data can distort the accuracy and relevance of the information reported to the public. The market for energy derivatives also has changed in other ways. Specifically, trading has grown on other markets, namely, exempt commercial markets—electronic trading facilities that trade exempt commodities, more than half of which trade in energy products—and OTC markets.[6] Currently, CFTC receives limited information on derivatives trading on exempt commercial markets—for example, records of allegations or complaints of suspected fraud or manipulation, and price, quantity, and other data on contracts that average five or more trades a day. The commission may receive limited information from OTC participants, such as trading records, to help CFTC enforce the CEA's antifraud or antimanipulation provisions. The scope of CFTC's oversight authority with respect to these markets has raised concerns among some Members of Congress and others that activities on these markets are largely unregulated, and that additional CFTC oversight is needed. While many regulators have resisted calls for more regulation in the past, recent events in the physical and energy derivatives markets have resulted in renewed focus on the sufficiency of CFTC's authority. As a result, CFTC held a hearing in September 2007 to begin examining trading on regulated exchanges and exempt commercial markets. The hearing included assessments of the relationship between these markets and assessments of whether markets other than NYMEX serve a price discovery function, which is the process of determining a commodity's price on the basis of supply and demand. These and future deliberations may provide insights into whether changes are needed in the scope of CFTC's authority. Depending on what CFTC finds in its assessments of the markets, Congress might want to consider what actions, if any, are warranted.

To detect fraudulent or abusive trading practices involving exchange-traded energy futures, CFTC daily monitors the trading on exchanges such as NYMEX. CFTC examines daily electronic trading data on futures contracts and other information sources, such as commercial sources on energy commodities and tips from individuals on possible violations. CFTC's surveillance program primarily relies on daily reports from large traders to detect problems, such as the potential for manipulation. When CFTC staff detect potential problems or violations, they may gather additional information from NYMEX officials, traders, or other sources to determine if further action is warranted. CFTC staff said that they routinely investigated traders with large open positions. However, the staff added that they did not routinely maintain information about such inquiries; instead they documented their actions only when further action was warranted. This lack of information makes it difficult to determine the usefulness and extent of these activities. Without sufficient data on these and other inquiries, CFTC's records will understate the extent to which the commission surveils trading activity. In addition, CFTC management also might miss opportunities both to identify trends in activities or markets and to better target its limited resources. According to information provided by CFTC, the commission coordinates its enforcement actions with NYMEX as well as FERC, DOJ, and others. It also has taken enforcement actions in cases of attempted manipulation and other abusive practices in energy derivatives trading that resulted in fines of $305 million from 2001 through 2005. While these cases have been successfully pursued, it is difficult to determine whether they have helped deter market manipulation or the other abusive practices these pursuits addressed because the effectiveness of enforcement activities is not easily measured. The Office of Management and Budget (OMB) has concluded that the enforcement program lacks performance measures that illustrate whether it is meeting its overall objective.

This report includes a matter for congressional consideration and three recommendations. In light of recent developments in derivatives markets and as part of CFTC's reauthorization process, Congress should consider further exploring whether the current regulatory structure for energy derivatives, in particular for those traded in exempt commercial markets, provides adequately for fair trading and accurate pricing of energy commodities. Our three recommendations to the Acting CFTC Chairman are aimed at improving the usefulness of information that CFTC provides to the public as a result of its surveillance activities and the efficiency of its enforcement program. First, we recommend that CFTC reexamine the classifications in the COT reports to determine if the commercial and noncommercial categories should be refined to improve the transparency, accuracy, and relevance of public information on trading activity in the energy futures markets. Second, we recommend that CFTC explore ways to routinely maintain written records of inquiries into possible improper trading activity and the results of these inquiries to more fully determine the usefulness and extent of its surveillance, antifraud, and antimanipulation authorities. Third, we recommend that CFTC examine ways to more fully demonstrate the effectiveness of its enforcement activities by developing additional outcome-related performance measures that more fully reflect progress on meeting the program's overall goals.

We provided a draft of this report to CFTC, and the commission provided written comments that are reprinted in appendix V. In its comments, CFTC generally agreed with our findings. CFTC said that the commission will reexamine classifications in the COT reports. CFTC also said that the commission will explore additional recordkeeping procedures for staff, but that it must balance the time required for such additional tasks against the need to undertake market surveillance by an already-stretched surveillance staff. CFTC added that it has included the development of measures to evaluate the effectiveness of its enforcement program in its most recent strategic plan. CFTC also provided technical comments, which we have incorporated in this report as appropriate.

BACKGROUND

Energy commodities are bought and sold in several different physical and financial markets. Physical markets include the spot, or cash, markets where products such as crude oil or gasoline are bought and sold for immediate or near-term delivery. The United States has several spot markets. Examples are the pipeline hub near Cushing, Oklahoma for West Texas Intermediate crude oil and the Henry Hub near Erath, Louisiana, for natural gas. The prices set in the specific spot markets provide a reference point that buyers and sellers use to set the price for other types of the commodity traded in other locations.

The prices established for energy commodities in the physical markets generally are determined by supply and demand. For example, when the demand for the product rises relative to supply because economies are growing, prices are likely to rise. Conversely, when demand falls relative to supply, prices are likely to fall. For energy products, demand and supply, and therefore price, can fluctuate on a seasonal basis. For example, consumer demand for gasoline in the United States is generally higher from May through early September—the summer driving season—and tends to flatten after Labor Day. Similarly, demand for natural gas and heating oil is highest during the heating season between October and March.

The relative inelasticity of energy commodities means that small shifts in demand and supply can result in relatively large price fluctuations. In general, when the price of an energy commodity rises, the demand for that product is likely to fall in the long term, and vice versa. However, demand for energy commodities is price inelastic in the short term—that is, the quantity demanded changes little in response to a change in price. On the supply side, rising energy commodities prices motivate producers to increase the amount of commodities they supply to increase profits.

However, because producers hold relatively low inventories of energy commodities in reserve, and finding and producing additional energy commodities takes a long time and is expensive, supply also is relatively inelastic. For example, supplies of natural gas from new production wells cannot be increased quickly to meet higher demand because of the time required to get the newly produced gas into the marketplace.

Energy commodities also are traded in the financial markets, especially in the form of derivatives. Derivatives include futures, options, and swaps, whose values are based on the performance of the underlying asset. Options give the purchaser the right, but not the obligation, to buy or sell a specific quantity of a commodity or financial asset at a designated price. Swaps traditionally are privately negotiated contracts that involve an ongoing exchange of one or more assets, liabilities, or payments for a specified period. Futures and options contracts are traded on exchanges designated by CFTC as contract markets (futures exchanges), where a wide range of energy, agricultural, financial, and other commodities are bought and sold for future delivery. Commodity futures and options can be traded on both OTC and exempt commercial markets if the transactions involve qualifying commodities and the participants satisfy statutory requirements.

Energy futures include standardized contracts for future delivery of a specific crude oil, heating oil, natural gas, or gasoline product at a particular spot market location. The exchange standardizes the contracts, and participants cannot modify them to their particular needs. For example, a standard gasoline futures contract traded on NYMEX is for 1,000 barrels (42,000 gallons), quoted in dollars and cents per gallon, and for delivery of up to 36 months into the future at New York Harbor.[7] The owner of an energy futures contract is obligated to buy or sell the commodity at a specified price and future date. However, the owner may eliminate the contractual obligation before the contract expires by selling or purchasing other contracts with terms that offset the original contract. In practice, relatively few futures contracts on NYMEX result in physical delivery of the underlying commodity, but instead are liquidated with offsets. Options on futures contracts also are traded on exchanges such as NYMEX and foreign boards of trade that U.S. traders access directly.

In addition to exchange-traded futures and options, the financial markets for energy commodities include derivatives traded among multiple traders on exempt commercial markets and derivatives created bilaterally in OTC transactions. As with futures, exempt commercial markets and other OTC derivatives allow producers and users of energy commodities to manage the risk of future changes in the price of a particular commodity. These contracts include options and swaps at an agreed-upon price. Appendix II shows some of the different types of contracts and transactions for energy commodities in the physical and financial markets.

Functions of Futures Markets

Market participants use futures markets to offset the risk caused by changes in prices, discover commodity prices, and speculate on price changes.

Some buyers and sellers of energy commodities in the physical markets trade in futures contracts to offset, or "hedge," the risks of price changes in the physical markets. The futures markets help buyers and sellers determine, or "discover," the price of commodities in the physical markets, thus linking the two markets. Other participants—generally, speculators—that do not have a commercial interest in the underlying commodities but are looking to make a profit take varying positions on the future value of commodities. In doing so, speculators provide liquidity and assume risks that other participants, such as hedgers, seek to avoid. Arbitrageurs are a third group of participants that aim to benefit by identifying discrepancies in price relationships, rather than by betting on future price movements. Arbitrage is a strategy that involves simultaneously entering into several transactions in multiple markets to benefit from price discrepancies across markets. For example, traders can trade simultaneously in exchanges and OTC.

Price risk is an important concern for buyers and sellers of energy commodities because wide fluctuations in cash market prices introduce uncertainty for producers, distributors, and consumers of commodities and make investment planning, budgeting, and forecasting more difficult. A statistical measurement of the degree to which prices fluctuate over time is known as "volatility" and can be applied to prices in both the physical and financial markets. There are two basic types of volatility measurements. Historical volatility measures are calculated on the basis of price changes, using data from market transactions. Implied volatility reflects market participants' expectations of future volatility as derived from the prices of traded options (see app. III). This report presents data on the relative historical volatility of energy futures contracts, which we calculated from relative changes in daily prices.

Futures and off-exchange derivatives markets provide participants with a means to hedge or shift unwanted price risk to others more willing to assume the risk or those having different risk situations. For example, if a petroleum refiner wanted to shed its risk of losing money as a result of falling gasoline prices, it could lock in a price by selling futures contracts to deliver the gasoline in 6 months at a guaranteed price. Likewise, a transportation company that knows it must refill its gasoline tanks in 6 months might want to offset the price risk associated with purchasing fuel by buying futures contracts to take delivery of gasoline then at a set price. Without futures contracts that help them manage risk, producers, refiners, and others likely would face uncertainty related to investment planning, budgeting, and forecasting—and potentially higher costs.

Futures markets also provide a means of price discovery for commodities such as energy products. For price discovery, markets need current information about supply and demand, a large number of participants, and transparency. Market participants monitor and analyze the factors that currently affect, and that they expect to affect, the future supply and demand for energy commodities. With that information, they buy or sell energy commodity contracts on the basis of the price for which they believe the commodity will sell at the delivery date. The futures markets, in effect, distill the diverse views of market participants into a single price. In turn, buyers and sellers of physical commodities consider those predictions about future prices with other factors when setting prices on the spot and retail markets.

A wide variety of participants hedge and speculate in energy derivatives markets. For the exchange-traded futures markets, CFTC categorizes traders in general terms as either commercial or noncommercial participants. CFTC identifies several subcategories of participants within the commercial category: producers, manufacturers, dealers/merchants, and swaps/derivatives dealers. Dealers and merchants include, among others, wholesalers, exporters and importers, shippers, and crude oil marketers. Typical noncommercial traders are entities such as those that manage money ("managed money traders").[8] These noncommercial traders include, among others, commodity pool operators (CPO) and commodity trading advisors (CTA), many of which advise or operate hedge funds.[9] Other noncommercial traders include floor brokers and unregistered traders.

Relationship between Futures and Spot Prices

The prices for energy commodities in the futures and in the spot or physical markets are closely linked because they are influenced by the same market fundamentals in the long run. Prices in the physical spot and futures markets for the four energy commodities we reviewed are highly correlated and rose dramatically from 2002 to 2006. As shown in Figure 1, from January 2002 to July 2006, monthly average spot prices for crude oil, gasoline, and heating oil increased by at least 220 percent.[10] Natural gas spot prices increased by more than 140 percent. At the same time that spot prices increased, the futures prices for these commodities showed a similar pattern of a sharp and sustained increase from January 2002 into 2006. For example, the price of crude oil futures increased from an average of $22 per barrel in January 2002 to an average of $74 per barrel in July 2006. Natural gas futures prices spiked rapidly in the fall of 2005 after several strong hurricanes raised concerns about supply disruptions for the winter of 2005-2006, then prices fell sharply due in part to a mild winter. Prices in the spot and futures markets show similar patterns because traders in those markets tend to rely on the same types of information when entering into transactions.

The differences between futures and spot market prices for energy commodities narrow and the prices converge when futures contracts near expiration and physical delivery is required. As the expiration date nears, the physical delivery provision of the contract and the ability of traders to arbitrage combine to bring the futures and physical market prices together. Arbitrage plays a crucial role in moderating or removing price differences between spot and futures markets and contributes to the convergence of futures and spot prices at expiration. For example, if the price for a crude oil futures contract that would expire in 2 weeks were $62 per barrel and the spot market price were $60 per barrel, a trader could choose to buy oil now at the spot price and enter into a futures contract to deliver oil in 2 weeks at the futures price, thereby making a $2 profit.[11] This and similar transactions by other traders would put upward pressure on the spot price and downward pressure on the futures price and move them toward convergence. Figure 2 provides an example of how the price of the April 2006 crude oil futures contract and the spot price for that commodity converged as the contract approached expiration.

Changes in CFTC Oversight Authority and Resource Levels

Between the creation of CFTC in 1974 and the year 2000, the CEA generally restricted commodity derivatives trading to futures and options entered into on exchanges and made all transactions in futures contracts subject to CFTC's exclusive jurisdiction. However, in the late 1980s and early 1990s, commercial entities began entering into nonstandardized, off-exchange derivative contracts that had pricing characteristics similar to futures (i.e., pricing of the transactions derived from the prices of various commodities), and the instruments were used for risk shifting. According to CFTC officials, under exemptive authority provided in 1992 reauthorization legislation, CFTC announced that it would not take enforcement action against qualified commercial entities engaged in certain types of energy derivatives transactions, but the legality of instruments not covered by the exemption (i.e., their status as futures contracts subject to the CEA) remained unresolved.[12]

In 2000, the CFMA amended the CEA to provide for both regulated markets and markets largely exempt from regulation and to permit off-exchange trading of energy derivatives by qualified parties.[13] The regulated markets include futures exchanges that have self-regulatory surveillance and monitoring responsibilities as self-regulatory organizations (SRO) and by CFTC.[14] CFTC's primary mission includes preserving the integrity of these futures markets and protecting market users and the public from fraud, manipulation, and abusive practices related to the sale of commodity futures and options. This mission is achieved through a regulatory scheme that is based on federal oversight of industry self-regulation. The CEA also permits derivatives trading in markets that are largely exempt from CFTC's regulatory authority, including both OTC and exempt commercial markets, subject to statutory requirements governing the types of commodity and trader and the facility used for conducting the trades. The President's Working Group's 1999 report on OTC derivatives focused on changes to the CEA that in their view would "promote innovation, competition, efficiency, and transparency in OTC derivatives markets, to reduce systemic risk, and to allow the United States to maintain leadership in these rapidly developing markets."[15] Derivatives on energy commodities, which are within the act's definition of "exempt commodity," may be traded in exempt commercial markets by eligible commercial entities, a category of traders broadly defined in the CEA to include firms with a commercial interest in the underlying commodity as well as other sophisticated investors, such as hedge funds. Violations of the CEA and CFTC regulations may be remedied by imposition of civil monetary penalties, trading bans, restitution, and other appropriate relief.

In addition to CFTC oversight, futures exchanges accept self-regulatory obligations as a condition of designation. For example, NYMEX, as an SRO, is responsible for establishing and enforcing rules governing member conduct and trading; providing for the prevention of market manipulation, including monitoring trading activity; ensuring that futures industry professionals meet qualifications; and examining exchange members for financial soundness and other regulatory purposes. CFTC oversees SROs to ensure that each has an effective self-regulatory program.[16]

Within CFTC, three of the commission's six major operating units actively oversee futures exchanges and their derivatives clearing organizations.[17]

- The Division of Market Oversight approves and oversees the futures exchanges, conducts its own market surveillance, conducts trade practice reviews and investigations, and reviews exchange rules.

- The Division of Clearing and Intermediary Oversight oversees, among other things, derivatives clearing organizations and the registration of intermediaries, which are persons such as futures commission merchants, CPOs, or CTAs that act on the behalf of others in futures trading.18
- The Division of Enforcement investigates and prosecutes alleged violations of the CEA and CFTC regulations.

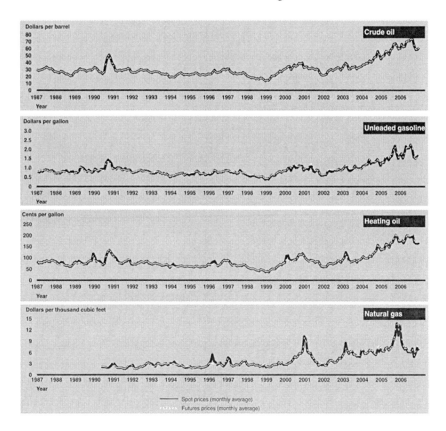

Figure 1. Monthly Average Spot Prices and Front Month Futures Settlement Prices, in Constant 2006 Dollars, 1987–2006 Dollars

Source: GAO analysis of Global Insight and NYMEX data.

Note: The front month futures contract is the actively traded contract with the closest delivery date. NYMEX did not begin trading natural gas futures until 1990.

Figure 2. Convergence of the April 2006 Crude Oil Futures Contract Price and the
Crude Oil Spot Price, March 22, 2004–March 21, 2006

Source: GAO analysis of EIA and NYMEX data

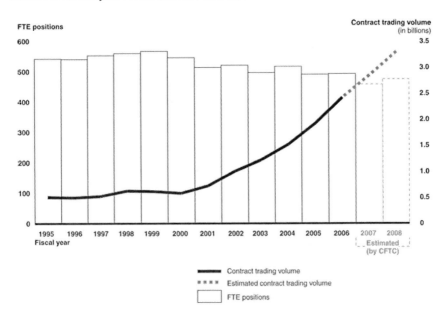

Figure 3. Futures and Options Trading Volume for All Commodities and CFTC
Staffing Levels (Actual and Estimated), Fiscal Years 1995–2008

Source: GAO analysis of CFTC, the National Finance Center, and the Futures Industry Association data.

At the beginning of fiscal year 2006, 167 (34 percent) of CFTC's 490 full-time-equivalent (FTE) positions were allocated to the first two CFTC divisions; at the beginning of fiscal year 2007, that allocation declined to 162 (35 percent) of CFTC's 458 FTE positions. These staff monitor the markets and market participants from CFTC's headquarters in Washington, D.C., as well as from field offices in New York; Chicago; Kansas City; and, until recently, Minneapolis.[19] About one-third of CFTC's staff are located in the field offices. At the beginning of fiscal year 2006, 132 (27 percent) of CFTC's 490 FTE positions were allocated to the Division of Enforcement; at the beginning of fiscal year 2007, that number declined to 120 of CFTC's 458 FTE positions. The 2007 data are estimated. While CFTC staffing levels have declined, according to CFTC, futures and options trading volume for all commodities has roughly doubled from fiscal years 2002 to 2006 and is expected to continue to rise, as indicated in Figure 3.

SEVERAL FACTORS HAVE CAUSED CHANGES IN THE ENERGY MARKETS, POTENTIALLY AFFECTING PRICES

Both physical and futures markets experienced a substantial amount of change from 2002 through 2006. Reasonable arguments have been made that events in both markets have contributed to rising energy prices, at least in the short term, but opinions vary regarding the extent that recent changes in the financial markets have influenced the prices of energy products in the physical markets over the long term. Because of these concurrent changes, identifying the causes of the increases in energy prices in both the physical and futures markets for crude oil, unleaded gasoline, heating oil, and natural gas is difficult. First, during this period, the physical markets experienced tight supply and rising demand from increasing global demand, ongoing political instability in oil-producing regions, and other supply disruptions. Second, annual volatility of energy prices remained above historic averages during the beginning of the period (although during 2006, volatility generally declined to levels at or near the historical average). Third, the volume of trading in energy futures increased as growing numbers of managed money traders viewed energy futures as attractive investment alternatives.

Tight Supply and Rising Demand for Physical Energy Commodities Contributed to the Increase in Futures and Spot Prices

The energy physical markets have undergone substantial change and turmoil from 2002 through 2006, which affected prices in the spot and futures markets. First, like many market observers and participants, we found a number of fundamental supply and demand conditions that could influence prices. Moreover, these parties have observed that the lack of spare capacity in certain areas, such as production, transportation, and storage, can affect prices. Second, over the short term, weather events also were a significant cause of rising energy prices because of their effects on energy supply, according to several of the market observers we interviewed. Third, many market observers also identified geopolitical uncertainty arising from the instability and insecurity of the world's major oil-producing regions as a major factor affecting energy prices.[20] Concerns about political events may manifest in the form of higher futures prices if traders predict that an event—such as a strike within the industry or pipeline sabotage by terrorists—will have an effect on future supply. Finally, on the demand side, a significant factor noted by observers was the increase in global consumption of petroleum products, primarily among industrializing Asian nations such as China and India.

Analysis of world oil prices by EIA and us indicates that increases in crude oil prices occur if political instability, terrorist acts, or natural disasters create uncertainties about, or actual disruptions in, supply from countries that produce or refine oil. For example, according to EIA, in the early 2000s, cutbacks in the Organization of the Petroleum Exporting Countries (OPEC) production and rising demand caused oil prices to increase to more than $30 per barrel, only to fall precipitously when the global economy weakened following the September 11, 2001, crisis.[21] Moreover, as we reported in 2005, rapid growth in oil demand in Asia contributed to a rise in crude oil prices to more than $50 per barrel during 2004.[22]

According to EIA, world oil demand that was about 59 million barrels per day in 1983 grew to more than 85 million barrels per day in 2006. The United States consumes nearly one-quarter of this amount—or more than 20 million barrels per day in 2006—and its demand has grown about 1.5 percent per year since 1983. The rapid economic growth in Asia also has stimulated a strong demand for energy commodities. For example, China has overtaken Japan as the second-largest consumer of crude oil, after the United States. According to EIA data, from 1983 to 2004, Chinese demand grew from about 1.7 million barrels consumed per day to about 6.4 million barrels consumed per day. This increase in the global demand for crude oil is shown in Figure 4.

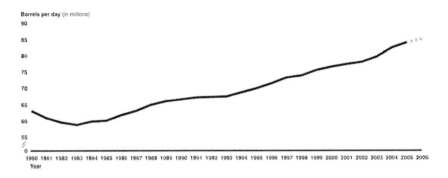

Figure 4. Increase in World Demand for Crude Oil (Actual and Estimated), 1980–2006

Source: GAO analysis of EIA data.
Note: The world oil demand data for 2006 represent a preliminary estimate.

The growth in demand does not, by itself, lead to higher prices for crude oil or any other energy commodity. For example, if the growth in demand were exceeded by a growth in supply, prices would fall, with other things remaining constant. However, according to EIA, the growth in demand outpaced the growth in supply, even with spare production capacity included in supply. Spare production capacity is surplus oil that can be produced and brought to the market relatively quickly to rebalance the market if there were a supply disruption anywhere in the world oil market. EIA estimates that global spare production capacity in 2006 was about 1.3 million barrels per day (see Figure 5). Most of that capacity was concentrated in the 12 OPEC countries that supply about 40 percent of the world's oil, primarily Saudi Arabia. This compared with spare capacity of about 10 million barrels per day in the mid-1980s, or of about 5.6 million barrels a day as recently as 2002. Analysis by EIA indicates that the growth of oil production in non-OPEC nations, which produce most of the world's oil and include countries such as Canada, China, Mexico, Norway, Russia, the United Kingdom, and the United States, has slowed relative to the growth in demand, and these nations have virtually no spare production capacity. As a commodity that is produced and traded worldwide, crude oil prices could be affected by the value of the U.S. dollar on open currency markets. For example, because crude oil is typically denominated in U.S. dollars, the payments that oil-producing countries receive for their oil also are denominated in U.S. dollars. As a result, a weak U.S.

dollar decreases the value of the oil sold at a given price, and oil-producing countries may wish to increase prices for their crude oil to maintain purchasing power in the face of a weakening U.S. dollar, to the extent they can.

Major weather and political events also can lead to supply disruptions and higher prices. In its analysis, EIA has cited the following examples:

- Hurricanes Katrina and Rita removed about 450,000 barrels per day from the world oil market from June 2005 to June 2006.
- Instability in major OPEC oil-producing countries, such as Iran, Iraq, Nigeria, and Venezuela, has lowered production and increased the risk of future production shortfalls.
- Oil production in Russia, a major driver of non-OPEC supply growth during the early 2000s, was adversely affected by a worsened investment climate as the government raised export and extraction taxes.

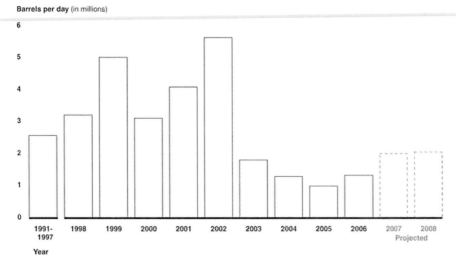

Figure 5. Estimates of World Oil Spare Production Capacity, 1991–2008

Source: GAO analysis of EIA data.
Note: The spare production capacity data for 1991–1997 represent an average estimate over that period.

The supply of crude oil affects the supply of gasoline and heating oil, and, just as production capacity affects the supply of crude oil, refining capacity affects the supply of products distilled from crude oil. As we have reported, refining capacity in the United States has not expanded at the same pace as the demand for gasoline.[23] Despite a growth in the capacity of existing gasoline refineries, the growth in demand has meant that refineries have been running at an average of more than 93 percent of production capacity since the mid-1990s, compared with about 78 percent in the 1980s. Higher utilization rates can increase operating costs and lead to prices being higher than otherwise would be expected, as occurred in the second half of the 1990s.

Another factor affecting the supply, and therefore the price, of petroleum products is the amount held in inventory. Inventory is particularly crucial to the supply and demand balance because it can provide a cushion against price spikes if, for example, a refinery outage temporarily disrupts production. We have reported that, as in other industries, the petroleum products industry has adopted "just-in-time" delivery processes to reduce costs, leading to a downward trend in the level of gasoline inventories in the United States. For example, in the early 1980s, private companies held stocks of gasoline in excess of 35 days of average U.S. consumption; while in 2004, those stocks were equivalent to less than 25 days consumption.[24] Lower costs of holding inventories may reduce gasoline prices, but lower levels of inventories also may cause prices to be more volatile because when a supply disruption occurs or there is an increase in demand, there are fewer stocks of readily available gasoline from which to draw, thereby putting upward pressure on prices. Others have noted that higher prices for future delivery of oil have induced oil companies to buy more oil and place it in storage. They concluded that this practice has created a situation where oil prices are high despite high levels of oil in inventory.

In addition to the supply and demand factors that generally apply to all energy commodities, there are specific conditions that apply to particular commodities. For example, to meet national air quality standards under the Clean Air Act, as amended, many states have mandated the use of special gasoline blends—so-called "boutique fuels." As we have recently reported, there is a general consensus that higher costs associated with supplying special gasoline blends contributed to higher gasoline prices, either because of more frequent or more severe supply disruptions or because higher costs are likely passed on, at least in part, to consumers.[25] As another example, according to EIA, the recent phaseout of a chemical used to improve gasoline performance—methyl tertiary butyl ether—increased the price of U.S. gasoline, in part because the chemical was replaced by ethanol, a more costly additive. As in the futures markets, the physical markets have undergone substantial changes that can affect prices. These specific factors affecting particular commodities, when combined with the general supply and demand conditions, contribute to increased energy prices and price volatility. However, market participants and other observers disagree on whether high energy prices were solely due to supply and demand fundamentals or whether increased futures trading activity also was fueling higher prices.

The Effects of Relatively High but Falling Volatility and a Growing Volume of Derivatives Trading on Energy Prices Are Unclear

The changes occurring in the physical markets have not happened in isolation; they have been accompanied by advances in technology, relatively high but falling volatility in energy futures prices, and a growing volume of trading in the derivatives markets. The effects of these changes on energy prices are not clear.

Although energy futures prices increased from 2002 to 2006 (see Figure 1), the relative volatility of those prices for three of the four commodities generally declined. As shown in figure 6, the annual historical volatilities— measured using the relative change in daily prices of energy futures—from 2000 through 2006 generally were above or near their long-term averages, although crude oil and heating oil declined below the average and gasoline declined slightly. As we have reported, futures prices typically reflect the effects of such world events on the price of crude oil.[26] Political instability and terrorist acts in countries that supply oil create uncertainties about future supplies, which is reflected in futures prices in anticipation of an oil shortage and expected higher prices in the future. Conversely, news about a new oil discovery that would increase world oil supply could result in lower futures prices. In other words, futures traders' expectations of what may happen to world oil supply and demand influence their price decisions.

The annual volatility of natural gas fluctuated more widely than that of the other three commodities and increased in 2006, even though prices largely declined from the levels reached in 2005. EIA has stated that the volatility of natural gas prices is due to factors in the physical marketplace, such as changing weather, producers' inability to move natural gas quickly to areas in response to quickly rising demand, and limited local storage. A research director for a consumer advocacy organization who studied natural gas prices concluded that increased trading by speculators had increased volatility and prices.[27] CFTC also has studied this issue and found that natural gas prices from August 2003 through August 2004 did not appear to be determined by any single category of market participant, although joint demand and supply of contracts by all participants clearly affected the change in price. In other words, managed money traders' activity (including hedge funds), by itself, did not have a significant effect on price changes.[28]

While some often equate higher prices with higher volatility, an increase in futures contract prices does not necessarily mean that volatility will increase in a similar manner, and an increase in volatility does not necessarily mean that prices will rise. Price volatility measures the variability rather than the direction of price changes and is based on the standard deviation of those changes.[29] Therefore, if futures contract prices change at a steady rate, the prices may have lower volatility than if large swings in prices occurred.

At the same time that prices were rising and volatility was generally above or near long-term averages, futures markets also experienced an increase in the number of large noncommercial participants, such as managed money traders.[30] The trends in price and volatility made the energy derivatives markets attractive for an increasing number of traders looking to either hedge against those changes or profit from them. According to CFTC large trader data, from July 2003 to December 2006, crude oil futures and options contracts experienced the most dramatic increase as the average number of noncommercial traders grew from about 125 to about 286. As shown in Figure 7, over a similar period, the average number of noncommercial traders also showed an upward but less dramatic trend for unleaded gasoline, heating oil, and natural gas.

Some market participants and observers have concluded that large purchases of oil futures contracts by speculators in effect have created an additional demand for oil that has led to higher prices; others disagree. The Senate's Permanent Subcommittee on Investigations, Committee on Homeland Security and Governmental Affairs, issued a staff report in June 2006 that concluded that the traditional forces of supply and demand could not fully account for increases in the prices of energy commodities.[31] Also, according to an energy firm, an investment bank, an academic, and hedge fund officials, increasing numbers of speculative traders in the market and rising trading volume placed upward pressure on futures prices. However, others, including investment bank and CFTC officials, have argued that speculators did not increase prices, but they provided liquidity and dampened volatility. Moreover, other investment banks, energy firms, and FERC officials told us that speculative trading in the futures markets can contribute to short-term price movements in the physical markets. However, they did not believe it was possible to sustain a speculative "bubble" over time because the two markets are linked and both respond to information regarding changes in supply and demand caused by such factors as the weather or geopolitical events. Therefore, in their view, speculation could not lead to artificially high or low prices over a long period.

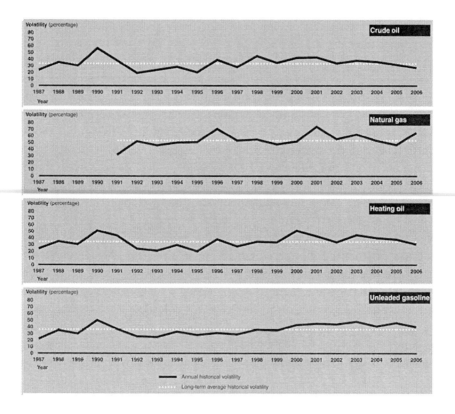

Figure 6. Comparison of Annual Volatility with the Long-term Average Volatility for Four Energy Futures (Measured in Relative Terms Using Front Month Contracts), 1987–2006

Source: GAO analysis of NYMEX data.
Note: NYMEX did not begin trading natural gas futures until 1990.

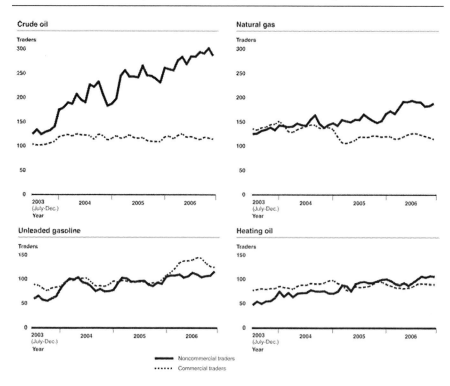

Figure 7. Average Daily Number of Large Commercial and Noncommercial Traders per Month, July 2003–December 2006

Source: GAO analysis of CFTC data.

Within the noncommercial trader category, the largest increases came from managed money traders—which generally trade for their own accounts rather than for others. Specifically, for crude oil, the average number of managed money traders that trade daily increased significantly from about 62 in July 2003 to about 128 in December 2006. At the same time, the number of smaller traders also grew significantly from an average of about 26 per day in July 2003 to an average of about 111 per day in December 2006. The number of managed money traders and smaller traders for unleaded gasoline, heating oil, and natural gas also increased similarly during that period. The number of commercial futures traders generally did not increase in a fashion similar to that of noncommercial traders.

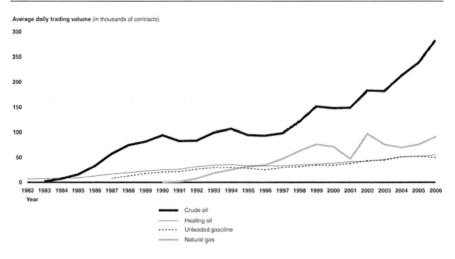

Figure 8. Average Daily Trading Volume for Crude Oil, Heating Oil, Unleaded Gasoline, and Natural Gas Futures Contracts, 1982–2006

Source: GAO analysis of NYMEX data.
Note: The trading volume data for unleaded gasoline include the RB contract introduced on NYMEX in October 2005. The start dates for these commodities varied for these NYMEX contracts.

As the number of traders has increased, so has the trading volume on NYMEX for all energy futures contracts, particularly crude oil and natural gas, as shown in Figure 8. From 2001 through 2006, the average daily contract volume for crude oil increased by 90 percent and for natural gas increased by 93 percent. However, unleaded gasoline and heating oil experienced less dramatic growth in their trading volumes during this period.

Along with the strong growth of energy futures trading, the amount of energy derivatives traded outside of exchanges also appears to have increased significantly. However, comprehensive data on the trading volume of energy-related OTC derivatives are not available because OTC energy markets are not regulated. The Bank for International Settlements publishes data on worldwide OTC derivative trading volume for broader groupings of commodities that can be used as a rough proxy for trends in the trading volume of OTC energy derivatives.[32] According to these data, the notional amounts outstanding of OTC commodity derivatives—excluding precious metals, such as gold—grew by 854 percent from December 2001 through December 2005.[33] From December 2004 through December 2005, the notional amount outstanding increased by 214 percent to more than $3.2 trillion. Despite the lack of comprehensive energy-specific data on OTC derivatives, the recent experience of individual trading facilities revealed the growth of energy derivatives trading outside of futures exchanges. For example, according to an annual financial statement of the IntercontinentalExchange (ICE), the volume of contracts traded on ICE—including financially settled derivatives and physical contracts—increased by 438 percent, from more than 24 million contracts in 2003 to more than 130 million in 2006.

While some market observers believed that managed money traders were exerting upward pressure on prices by predominantly buying futures contracts, CFTC data reveal that, from the middle of 2003 through the end of 2006, the trading activity of managed money participants became increasingly balanced between buying and selling. According to basic futures market theory, a trader speculating and holding an outstanding position to buy the commodity—a long open interest position—expects that the price of the commodity will rise, while a trader holding an outstanding position to sell the commodity—a short open interest position—expects that the price will decline. As shown in Figure 9, according to CFTC data, from July 2003 through December 2003 managed money traders' ratio of long open interest in crude oil to short open interest was about 2.5:1, suggesting a strong expectation that prices would rise, on average, throughout that period, which they did. By 2006, this ratio fell to 1.2:1, suggesting that managed money traders as a whole were more evenly divided in their expectations about future prices. Managed money trading in unleaded gasoline, heating oil, and natural gas showed similar trends. Although for natural gas, open interest was more often short than long, suggesting a general expectation that prices would decline, which largely did not occur until 2006. Also, the relatively high percentage of open interest for natural gas held by these traders in 2006—surging to just over 40 percent— was perhaps due to the increased volatility of natural gas futures prices from 2005 to 2006, which provided traders with more opportunities for profit (or loss).

CFTC OVERSEES EXCHANGES AND HAS LIMITED AUTHORITY OVER OTHER DERIVATIVES MARKETS

Energy products are traded on multiple markets, which are subject to varying levels of CFTC oversight and regulation. Under the CEA, CFTC regulatory oversight is focused on conducting the surveillance of futures exchanges, protecting the public, and ensuring market integrity. CFTC collects and analyzes trading position information on futures exchanges, which is central to this oversight. The information is subsequently published at highly aggregated levels in the commission's COT reports, and it helps to provide transparency to the market. However, these public reports have been criticized because the informational categories for traders do not accurately reflect energy market activity. While CFTC's oversight is focused on futures exchanges, the number of exempt commercial markets for trading energy commodities, which are not subject to general CFTC oversight, have grown. However, traders in these markets are subject to the CEA's antimanipulation and, where applicable, antifraud provisions.[34] Also, exempt commercial markets must provide CFTC with data for certain contracts and notify CFTC if cash markets use exempt market prices to price their transactions (although that has not occurred).[35] Energy products also are traded off exchange (referred to as OTC) and are not subject to direct CFTC oversight and regulation. However, as we have previously noted, certain types of off-exchange transactions are subject to antifraud and the antimanipulation provisions of the CEA, which CFTC has the authority to enforce. In addition, contract participants may be subject to other regulatory authority on the basis of their role in the physical market. To enhance its ability to detect and deter price manipulations, CFTC has published for comment a proposal to amend part 18 of its regulations to obtain from traders that have large (reportable) positions in an exchange-traded commodity information about their off-exchange positions in the same commodity.[36] CFTC also held a hearing in September 2007 to examine trading on regulated exchanges and exempt commercial markets, which included an assessment of price discovery and the implications for CFTC oversight.

CFTC Has General Oversight Authority over Futures Exchanges, but Its Publicly Reported Information on These Exchanges Has Not Kept Pace with Changing Market Conditions

Under the CEA, CFTC has general oversight authority over futures exchanges such as NYMEX. These exchanges receive CFTC approval to list futures and options contracts for trading and are subject to direct CFTC regulation and oversight. To be a regulated futures exchange, an exchange must demonstrate to CFTC that the exchange complies with (1) the criteria for designation under section 5(b) of the CEA for, among other things, the prevention of market manipulation, fair and equitable trading, the conduct of trading facilities, and the financial integrity of transactions conducted on the board; (2) the set of core principles under section 5(d) of the act establishing their regulatory responsibilities; and (3) the provisions on application procedures of part 38 of the CFTC rules.[37] According to CFTC officials, following procedures in the CEA, these exchanges may list new contracts, after certifying that they are in compliance with certain core principles, including ascertaining that the contracts are not readily susceptible to manipulation and monitoring trading to prevent price manipulation.[38]

CFTC's oversight is focused on fulfilling three strategic goals relating to futures exchanges. First, to ensure the economic vitality of the commodity futures and options markets, CFTC conducts its own direct market surveillance and also reviews on an oversight basis the surveillance efforts of these exchanges. According to CFTC officials, the commission monitors trading activity in futures markets and uses these trading data to analyze large positions that might be used to manipulate futures markets. In its oversight role, CFTC reviews new futures contracts to assess susceptibility to manipulation. To list a new futures contract, an exchange must file a written self-certification with CFTC and, if requested, must provide additional evidence, information, or data to CFTC on whether the contact satisfies CEA requirements and the commission's regulations or policies. Second, to protect market users and the public, CFTC has promoted sales practices and other customer protection rules applicable to futures commission merchants and other registered intermediaries.[39] In this connection, CFTC closely monitors the enforcement of registration and other requirements by the National Futures Association, which is an SRO responsible for regulating all firms and individuals conducting futures business with public customers. Third, to ensure the market's financial integrity, CFTC reviews the audit and financial surveillance activities of SROs. It also periodically reviews registered derivatives clearing organizations to ensure that they are effectively monitoring risks and protecting customer funds.

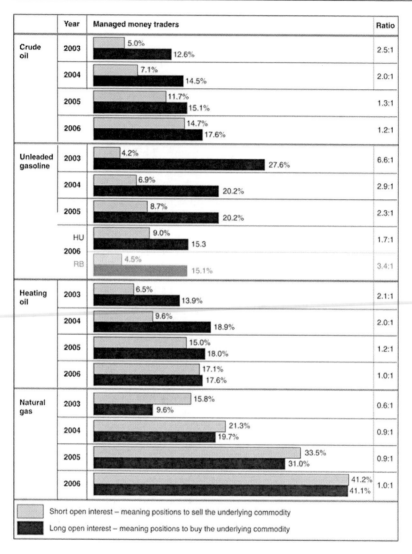

Figure 9. Percentage of Long and Short Open Interest in Futures and Options for Managed Money Traders, July 2003–December 2006 Page 31 GAO-08-25

Source: GAO analysis of CFTC data.

Note: Data for 2003 were for July through December. The percentages indicate what portion of long and short open interest was held by managed money traders. For example, in 2004, managed money traders held 14.5 percent of the total long open interest for crude oil and 7.1 percent of the total short open interest. Because data are not included for all categories of traders, the percentages for these categories within a particular period do not total 100. These data should be viewed as a general overview of managed money traders' positions. They do not provide insights into how traders' individual positions changed over time. Our data for 2006 include contract trading data for RB and for the gasoline—HU— that began to be replaced by RB.

CFTC provides the public information on open interest in exchange-traded futures and options by commercial and noncommercial traders for various commodities in its weekly COT reports, which are relied upon by the public. Changing market conditions caused CFTC in 2006 to reassess COT reporting and its value to the public.[40] A trading entity generally gets classified as commercial by filing a statement with CFTC that it is commercially "engaged in business activities hedged by the use of the futures or option markets." To ensure that traders are classified with accuracy and consistency, commission staff review this self-classification and may reclassify a trader if staff have additional information about the trader's use of the markets. A trader may be classified as commercial in some commodities and as noncommercial in other commodities. A single trading entity cannot be classified as both commercial and noncommercial in the same commodity. Nonetheless, a multifunctional organization that has more than one trading entity may have each trading entity classified separately in a commodity. For example, a financial organization trading in financial futures may have a banking entity whose positions are classified as commercial and have a separate money-management entity whose positions are classified as noncommercial.

Recently, CFTC observed that the exchange-traded derivatives markets, as well as derivatives trading patterns and practices, have evolved, leading CFTC to question whether the commercial and noncommercial categories of today's COT reports appropriately classify trading practices. In June 2006, CFTC issued a notice in the *Federal Register* that it was undertaking a comprehensive review of the COT reporting program out of concern that the reports in their present form might not accurately reflect the commercial or noncommercial nature of positions held by nontraditional hedgers, such as swaps dealers.[41] On the basis of the comments received in response to the notice, in December 2006, CFTC announced the initiation of a 2-year pilot program for publishing a supplemental COT report that would contain, in addition to categories for noncommercial and commercial positions, a category showing aggregate futures and options positions of index traders in 12 selected agricultural commodities. In explaining the program, CFTC observed that the "index traders" category would include traders that also were included in the noncommercial and commercial categories:

> "In addition, the Commission will begin publishing a supplemental COT report that includes, in a separate category, the positions of commodity index traders in certain physical commodity futures markets. These so-called 'Index Traders' will be drawn from both the current Noncommercial and the

Commercial categories. Coming from the Noncommercial category will be managed funds, pension funds and other institutional investors that generally seek exposure to commodity prices as an asset class in an unleveraged and passively managed manner using a standardized commodity index. Coming from the Commercial category will be entities whose positions predominantly reflect hedging of OTC transactions involving commodity indices—for example, swap dealers holding long futures positions to hedge short OTC commodity index exposure opposite institutional traders such as pension funds. These latter position holders are those traders described in the request for comments as 'non-traditional commercials.'"

CFTC stated that the pilot program for reporting of commodity index trading did not include energy and metals markets because the large trader data currently available to the commission would not permit an accurate breakout of index trading in these markets. According to CFTC, swap dealers, who use futures markets to hedge commodity index transactions in the OTC market, conduct most trading of commodity index-related futures. However, these swap dealers also may engage in OTC derivative transactions on energy or metals prices directly and conduct cash transactions in the underlying energy or metals markets. As a result of these activities, the overall futures positions held by swap dealers in energy and metal futures markets may not necessarily correspond closely with the hedging of OTC commodity index transactions. The commission stated that including these traders in the new index trader category would not enhance market transparency. Furthermore, it did not want to delay publication of the new COT report while it continues to study whether it is feasible to publish meaningful reports for other markets. The objective of the pilot program is to improve the transparency of an evolving market by separately reporting the positions of index traders. Similarly, the increasing volume of off-exchange trading in energy derivatives and the recent volatility of energy commodity prices justify considering whether a COT category of futures positions held by participants in off-exchange energy markets also could enhance transparency. CFTC said it will assess the relevance and usefulness of the new reporting and study whether it is possible and appropriate to expand the supplemental report to include data for other physical commodity futures markets.

Significant changes in the energy markets also may lead CFTC to further examine the usefulness, accuracy, and relevance of reported information to users. According to CFTC officials, energy trading has seen the entry of new market participants. For example, investment banks, hedge funds, and swaps dealers have become significant market participants. Moreover, according to industry analysts and representatives from investment banks and large oil companies, some commercial participants only hedge, some only speculate, and others both hedge and speculate in the energy markets. While some commercial participants may hedge and speculate in the same energy market, CFTC classifies these entities as commercial participants. CFTC has not been able to identify new categories for traders of energy commodities. Such reporting can distort the accuracy and relevance of reported information to users and the public, thereby limiting the usefulness of the information reported to the public as well as information used by traders.

CFTC Authority over Exempt Commercial Markets Consists of Enforcing the Antifraud and Antimanipulation Provisions of the CEA and Administering Certain Reporting Requirements

In contrast to the direct oversight provided to futures exchange, exempt commercial markets are not subject to CFTC's general oversight authority. According to CFTC officials, as these markets have grown in prominence, some market observers have questioned their role in the energy markets. Trading energy derivatives on exempt commercial markets is permissible only for eligible commercial entities. While not subject to general CFTC oversight, these markets are subject to CFTC rule 36.3, which provides for the dissemination of exempt commercial market trading data should exempt commercial market prices be used to price cash markets and contains notification, recordkeeping, and reporting requirements.[42] Also, exempt commercial market participants are subject to CFTC's enforcement authority for the antimanipulation and antifraud provisions of the CEA.[43] These markets are not required to register with CFTC, but must notify CFTC that they are operating as an exempt commercial market and comply with certain CFTC informational, recordkeeping, and other requirements.[44]

Specifically, CFTC promulgated rule 36.3 under two subsections of the CEA. One subsection authorizes CFTC to prescribe rules if necessary to ensure the timely dissemination of price, trading volume, and other trading data for a derivative traded on an exempt commercial market if the commission determines that the electronic trading facility used by the market performs a significant price discovery function for transactions in the cash market for the commodity underlying the derivative.[45] The other subsection establishes notification, recordkeeping, and reporting requirements for exempt commercial markets.[46] The rule requires, among other things, that the electronic trading facility in an exempt commercial market must notify CFTC of its reliance on the exemption and provide CFTC with price, quantity, and other data on contracts that average five or more trades a day over the most recent quarter for which they are relying on the CEA exemption. The facility also must maintain a record of allegations or complaints they receive concerning instances of suspected fraud or manipulation and provide CFTC with a copy of the record. CFTC officials said that the reports include transaction-level data, such as quantity and price, for all trades in products meeting the criteria, but not the identities of counterparties to the trades. These officials said that three exempt commercial markets—ICE, the Natural Gas Exchange, and ICAP—currently provide the rule 36.3 trade information reports; in the past, the Optionable and ChemConnect exempt commercial markets also provided these reports. For example, ICE officials told us that for their OTC activities they keep records for all of the products traded on their platform, and report to CFTC on liquid markets (those averaging five trades a day) and any complaints received from market participants. ICE officials said that CFTC often asks ICE for detailed information about participants that are putting up bids and offers and about all of the trades executed in a day.

CFTC officials said that the other electronic exchanges have provided notice that they are operating in reliance on the CEA exemption, but they have not provided rule 36.3 trade information reports. CFTC officials explained that an electronic exchange only has to provide information reports if it meets the threshold for reporting, which includes averaging five trades per day in the relevant contract. These officials also said that they do not actively check to determine whether the thresholds are being met.

To date, no exempt commercial market or CFTC has determined if cash markets for energy commodities routinely use exempt market prices to price their transactions. According to CFTC officials, an exempt commercial market or CFTC may determine, using certain criteria, if the market serves such a price discovery function. Exempt markets that serve such a function become subject to certain public reporting requirements. According to CFTC officials, the commission has not made such a determination for two reasons. First, they said that the only consequence of serving a price discovery function under current law is that the exempt commercial market must publish its prices. They noted that this is a circular argument because it is the public availability of pricing information that enables the exempt commercial market to serve a price discovery function. Second, they said that this is a low priority. In their view, the current fiscal situation does not allow CFTC to send its economists into the field on matters such as this that would not go before the commission.

Also in their view, even if the markets served a price discovery function, no significant consequence would entail because of the circularity argument. However, in light of the growth of trading on ICE and the lessons learned from the Amaranth crisis, CFTC held a hearing in September 2007 to examine trading on regulated exchanges and exempt commercial markets.[47] The hearings included an assessment of price discovery in these markets and the implications for CFTC oversight of these markets.

Table 1. Exempt Commercial Markets, Dates They Filed Notice with CFTC to Operate as an Exempt Commercial Market, and Commodities Traded on Each Market, 2001–2006

Notification date	Exempt commercial market	Commodity category
2006	ChemConnect	Energy products
2003	Chicago Climate Exchange	Emission allowances
2002	Commodities Derivative Exchange	Metals
2002	HoustonStreet Exchange	Energy products
2006	ICAP Commodity and Commodity Derivatives Trading System	Energy products
2006	ICAP Electronic Trading Community	Natural gas and its derivatives
2005	ICAP Hyde Limited Trading System	Forward freight agreements
2001	IntercontinentalExchange	Precious metals, base metals, and energy products
2001	International Maritime Exchange	Freight rates
2002	Natural Gas Exchange	Energy products
2006	NetThruPut	Condensates and liquefied petroleum gas
2001	Optionable	Energy products
2003	Spectron Live.com Limited	Liquefied petroleum gas
2003	TFS Energy	Weather derivatives
2005	Trade Capture	Energy products
2002	Tradespark	Energy products, weather indexes, and emission allowances
2003	Tradition Financial Services Pulp and Paper Division	Pulp and paper products

Source: GAO analysis of CFTC data.

Since 2001, 17 facilities have notified CFTC that they had begun operating as exempt commercial markets (see table 1). According to CFTC officials, 11 of these markets currently offer, or had offered, transactions in energy products, with 8 now operational. Some of these markets have become important players in the trading of energy products. ICE, in addition to the exempt swap contracts it trades in its capacity as an exempt commercial market, is the trading platform for physical commodities, including spot and forward contracts, which routinely involve delivery. According to CFTC officials, some in the industry assert that ICE is the trading platform for an estimated 70 percent of the spot trading for natural gas.[48] Another exempt commercial market, ChemConnect, advertises that data and news providers, such as Bloomberg and Dow Jones Energy Services, rely on it to provide accurate, timely information on energy products. Furthermore, the Web site for the HoustonStreet Exchange indicates that it serves as an electronic trading facility for crude oil and refined products also traded on NYMEX. While there has been significant growth in the number of electronic exchanges, CFTC officials said that they receive trade information reports from only 2—ICE and the Natural Gas Exchange. According to CFTC officials, they have no evidence that the others meet the minimum threshold trading volume for reporting.

Although CFTC Can Enforce Antimanipulation and Applicable Antifraud Provisions of the CEA in OTC Energy Derivatives Markets and Exempt Commercial Markets, Views Vary about the Sufficiency of Its Regulatory Authority with Respect to Off-Exchange Energy Derivatives

Energy derivatives also may be traded OTC, under the conditions and restrictions in the CEA for exempt commodities. The act exempts from most of its provisions transactions in exempt commodities into which large market participants enter and that are not traded on a trading facility. In addition, the act exempts from most of its provisions transactions in exempt commodities traded on an electronic trading facility, as long as large commercial traders (defined in the act as "eligible commercial entities") enter into them on a principal-to-principal basis.[49] Bilateral OTC derivatives contacts are viewed as private transactions between sophisticated counterparties, and there is no requirement for parties involved in OTC transactions to disclose details of their transactions. Because OTC derivatives are contractual agreements, each party is subject to and assumes the risk of nonperformance by its counterparty. This is different from exchange-traded derivatives, where a central clearinghouse stands behind every trade. Thus, according to officials of the International Swaps and Derivatives Association, in the OTC context it is vitally important that one has confidence in the creditworthiness and trustworthiness of one's counterparty. While these markets generally are not subject to direct CFTC oversight, CFTC has the authority to enforce antifraud and antimanipulation provisions of the CEA in connection with transactions in exempt commodities that take place through an electronic trading facility, and that are entered bilaterally without being subject to negotiation.[50] Several of the enforcement actions filed by CFTC since 2001 addressed the use of false reporting in an attempt to manipulate energy prices on NYMEX.

In addition to being subject to certain provisions of the CEA, the participants in these contracts may be subject to other regulatory authorities on the basis of their activities in the physical market. For example, certain actions—such as the buying and selling of a physical energy commodity by traders, such as hedge funds—may fall under the regulatory authority of FERC, which regulates the interstate transmission of physical commodities, such as natural gas, oil, and electricity, to protect energy consumers. Also, certain OTC derivative activities conducted by commercial banks are subject to oversight by the appropriate bank regulator. For example, commercial banks that engage in OTC derivatives are overseen by their relevant regulator, such as the Office of Comptroller of the Currency or the Board of Governors of the Federal Reserve System with respect to how their derivatives trading satisfies requirements of the banking laws. Likewise, SEC also has oversight authority over investment banks' activities that fall under its regulatory purview. These regulators do not regulate the specific transactions or maintain oversight of OTC derivatives as a class of instruments or markets; they regulate the entities that enter into the contracts or that act as dealers, counterparties, or both.

While some observers have called for more oversight of OTC derivatives, most notably for CFTC to be given greater oversight authority of this market, others oppose any such action as unnecessary. Supporters of more CFTC oversight authority believe that regulating OTC derivatives markets is needed to protect the regulated markets and protect consumers from potential abuse and possible manipulation. One of their concerns is that because there is little information available about the size of this market or the terms of the contracts, CFTC may not be assured that trading on the OTC market is not adversely affecting the regulated markets and, ultimately, consumers.

Specifically, some have mentioned that, unlike trading on a regulated exchange, OTC derivatives are not subject to any routine reporting requirements. Some have suggested that a combination of quantitative and qualitative information (such as whether derivatives are used mainly for trading or hedging purposes, and notional amounts by derivatives category) be collected.[51]

However others, including the President's Working Group, have concluded that OTC derivatives generally are not subject to manipulation because contracts are settled in cash on the basis of a rate or price determined in a separate, highly liquid market and these OTC transactions do not serve a significant price discovery function.[52] The Working Group also noted that if electronic markets were to develop and serve a price discovery function, then consideration should be given to enacting a limited regulatory regime aimed at enhancing market transparency and efficiency through CFTC, as the regulator of exchange-traded derivatives.

However, because of the lack of reported data about this market, addressing concerns about its function and effect on regulated markets and entities would be a challenge. CFTC officials have said that they have reason to believe these off-exchange activities affect prices determined on a regulated exchange. In a June 2007 *Federal Register* release clarifying its large trader reporting authority, CFTC noted that having data about the off-exchange positions of traders with large positions on regulated futures exchanges could enhance the commission's ability to deter and prevent price manipulation or any other disruptions to the integrity of the regulated futures markets.[53] According to CFTC officials, the commission also has proposed amendments to clarify its authority under the CEA to collect information and bring fraud actions in principal-to-principal transactions in these markets, thus enhancing CFTC's ability to enforce antifraud provisions of the CEA.[54]

Also, in August 2007, CFTC announced plans to conduct a hearing to begin examining more closely the trading on regulated exchanges and exempt commercial markets. The September 2007 hearing focused on a number of issues, including

- the current tiered regulatory approach established by the CFMA and whether this model is beneficial;
- the similarities and differences between exempt commercial markets and regulated exchanges, and the associated regulatory risks of each market; and

- the types of regulatory or legislative changes that might be appropriate to address any identified risks.

CFTC ENGAGES IN SURVEILLANCE ACTIVITIES AND ENFORCEMENT ACTIVITIES, BUT THE EFFECTIVENESS OF THESE ACTIVITIES IS LARGELY UNCERTAIN

CFTC provides oversight for commodity futures markets through routine surveillance, analysis of market data, and inquiries of market participants and others. The commission uses information gathered from surveillance activities to identify unusual trading activity and possible market abuse. In particular, CFTC's LTRS provides essential information for surveillance, and LTRS provides information on the majority of all trading activity on futures exchanges. CFTC staff also rely on data from other sources and on their experience to identify potential problems, reporting unresolved potential market problems to the commission. NYMEX also conducts its own surveillance activities. According to CFTC and industry officials, CFTC and NYMEX contact traders to collect additional information about questionable trading practices. CFTC staff also said that they routinely investigate traders with large open positions, but the staff added that they do not routinely maintain information about such inquiries, thereby making it difficult to determine the usefulness and extent of these activities. In addition, CFTC coordinates its surveillance activities with other federal, state, and foreign authorities. While CFTC's surveillance authority is limited to futures exchanges, the commission's enforcement authority for manipulation and fraud extends to both exchange-based trading and off-exchange trading in exempt commodities, such as energy products. According to data provided by CFTC, in recent years, it has used its enforcement authority to file enforcement actions for almost 300 cases, more than 30 of which involved energy-related commodities. However, as with programs operating in regulatory environments where performance is not easily measurable, evaluating the effectiveness of CFTC's enforcement activities is challenging because of the lack of effective outcome-based performance measures. CFTC's enforcement program received mixed ratings in a recent OMB review because CFTC could not fully demonstrate the effectiveness of its enforcement activities.

CFTC Oversight Includes Surveillance of Energy Futures Trading, but the Full Extent of Follow-up Activities Is Uncertain

CFTC conducts regular market surveillance and oversight of energy trading on NYMEX and other futures exchanges. These activities include focusing on detecting and preventing disruptive practices before they occur and keeping the CFTC commissioners informed of possible manipulation or abuse. In addition to conducting direct surveillance of trading in energy futures markets on NYMEX, CFTC focuses on NYMEX's compliance with appropriate CEA core principles, including monitoring of trading to prevent price manipulation and enforcing position limits and position accountability rules. In conducting its own surveillance activities, NYMEX may bring enforcement actions when violations are found. CFTC staff also investigate traders with large open positions and document cases of improper trading.

CFTC Oversees Trading on Futures Exchanges

According to CFTC officials, CFTC staff at three regional offices provide much of the market oversight and monitor daily trading activity. For instance, CFTC's New York Regional Office employs seven economists, who look for unusual trading and potential market manipulations in all futures contracts traded on New York futures exchanges. The New York regional staff obtain information from both market participants and NYMEX to monitor energy trading activity. New York CFTC staff stated that each morning, about 160 firms electronically submit large trader position data from the previous day to CFTC. CFTC headquarters receives these data and makes them available on a network to its field offices. Staff review these data for potential errors or omissions and then populate the LTRS, a database that staff use in conducting their surveillance activities.

CFTC staff also said that they rely on the commission's integrated surveillance system (ISS), which contains surveillance data that CFTC has collected from the futures exchanges, clearing members, foreign brokers, and large traders. According to CFTC's 2005 performance and accountability report, ISS is a critical application to support futures and options data market surveillance.55 This system provides continuously updated trading data on holders of large futures and option positions that CFTC staff uses daily to monitor futures and option trading, detect potential problems, and identify trends in the marketplace. According to CFTC officials, ISS also is used to facilitate analysis of data received from exempt markets as a result of special calls for information. For example, pursuant to separate special calls issued in

April, September, and December, 2006, ICE now continuously provides the commission with large trader position data. The commission also issued enforcement-related special calls seeking data for two individual ICE market participants in September 2006 and February 2007.

The LTRS, which is part of ISS, is a comprehensive system for collecting information on market participants, a key information source for CFTC's market surveillance program and essential for monitoring markets and identifying and resolving potential problems involving market congestion, manipulation, and speculative position limits.[56] Congestion may occur when traders holding short positions are attempting to cover their positions but are unable to find an adequate supply of contracts provided by traders with long positions or by new sellers willing to enter the market, except at sharply higher prices. In conducting their daily surveillance activities, CFTC officials said they analyze the trading data for indications that individual traders may be attempting to manipulate the market. This activity involves (1) looking for traders having unusually large market positions relative to open interest—the total number of futures contracts that have been entered into and not yet liquidated by an offsetting transaction or fulfilled by delivery—and deliverable supply and (2) examining the potential for disruption at expiration and sharp moves in the market. If certain positions pose concerns to CFTC staff, they can request additional information from a reporting firm or trader about trading and delivery activity.

CFTC staff also analyze trading using data from other sources. CFTC officials said that the staff look at price movements and price relationships—especially in the natural gas, crude oil, heating oil, and unleaded gasoline markets—using commercial information sources, such as Bloomberg, Gas Daily, Reuters, and other market sources. They also obtain information about traders by monitoring their Web sites and use NYMEX's and EIA's Web sites and Lexis-Nexis, as well as firms' Web sites. CFTC staff said that they are in regular contact with exchange officials, who have data on clearing members and trading activity. They also obtain surveillance information from other units within the commission and from tips by the public.

While CFTC data and other market collections are focused on identifying potential market disruptions and manipulations, staff also rely on their experience to identify potential problems. According to CFTC staff, the New York Regional Office staff assigned to surveillance of energy trading have many years of experience, either doing surveillance work for CFTC or in the futures industry, in general. Experienced staff are needed because, according to CFTC staff, analyzing market data is an art as well as a science. CFTC staff referred to the traditional test for manipulation set forth in the commission's *Indiana Farm* decision as a commonly recognized statement of the elements that are necessary to prove manipulation.[57]

According to CFTC staff, when a potential market problem has been identified, surveillance staff generally contact the exchange or traders to gather additional information. They said that surveillance staff may ask exchange employees, brokers, or traders questions to confirm positions and determine the intent of traders. They added that staff may express concern about the size of positions or possible actions by traders and caution traders to act responsibly.[58] According to the staff, CFTC's Division of Market Oversight may issue a warning letter or make a referral to the Division of Enforcement to conduct a nonpublic investigation into the trading activity. Markets where surveillance problems have not been resolved may be included in reports presented to the commission at weekly surveillance meetings. These reports provide information on traders with the four largest long and short positions; other market information, including delivery information; and background on the contact. According to CFTC staff, CFTC commissioners review the reports; discuss the situations with surveillance staff; and, if appropriate, consider other possible remedial actions, such as suggesting that the exchange take emergency action. If necessary, the commission itself may take emergency action.

If these actions do not resolve the issue or if an exchange fails to resolve a problem by taking actions that the commission deems appropriate, CFTC can order an exchange to take emergency actions. These actions include limiting trading, imposing or reducing limits on positions, requiring the liquidation of positions, extending a delivery period, or suspending trading. The commission has taken such emergency actions four times in its history, but never for energy markets.

In addition to CFTC's surveillance of NYMEX and trading on the exchange, NYMEX conducts its own surveillance activities and, if violations are found, brings its own enforcement actions. NYMEX is responsible for enforcing its own standards and CFTC's standards embodied in its rules governing the exchange, and its surveillance program is designed to monitor for possible manipulation by market participants. If NYMEX staff find potential violations, they will gather information and, if needed, take enforcement actions. For example, according to officials at a large refiner, NYMEX staff call them nearly every month about a large trade to make sure that their physical (or wet) barrels have moved and that their trade is not a price-setting mechanism or market ploy. Refiner officials added that even though NYMEX staff know they are a big refiner, they will examine their trades to see the actual signed contract to make sure it is valid. In their view, NYMEX staff are vigilant, as they should be. Officials from a hedge fund also said that both NYMEX and CFTC staff monitor their positions carefully and, as a speculator, would be notified immediately by NYMEX and CFTC if they were over the trading limits on any day. When asked about what weaknesses in the structure, monitoring, or enforcement mechanisms of derivative markets might allow for market manipulation, one market observer responded that he was not aware of any such weaknesses. Appendix III contains detailed discussion of NYMEX surveillance activities and enforcement actions.

Actions Taken by CFTC Staff to Inquire about Potential Problems May Not Always Be Documented

CFTC staff routinely make inquiries about traders with large open positions approaching expiration, but formal records of their findings are only kept in cases where there is evidence of improper trading. If LTRS data reveal that a trader has a large open market position that could disrupt markets if it were not closed before expiration, CFTC staff would contact the trader to determine why the trader had the position and what plans the trader had to close the position before expiration or to ensure that the trader was able to take delivery. If the traders provided a reasonable explanation for the position and a reasonable delivery or liquidation strategy, staff said that no further action would be required. CFTC staff said they would document such contacts on the basis of their importance in either informal notes, e-mails to supervisors, or informal memorandums. No formal record would be made of the inquiry, according to one CFTC official, unless there was a signal indicating improper trading activity. Without such data, CFTC's measures of the effectiveness of its actions to combat fraud and manipulation in the markets will not reflect this surveillance activity, and CFTC management might miss opportunities to both identify trends in activities or markets and better target its limited resources.

CFTC staff added that all surveillance projects and activities that require a minimum number of hours of work are tracked by quarterly statistical reports, including those futures expirations with large trader or deliverable supply problems. They said that expirations are routinely monitored by economists and reviewed with their supervisors through weekly surveillance reports. Economists are responsible for the analytical review of cash and futures market developments, including the assessment of supply and demand factors, basis and spread relationships, the adequacy of deliverable supply, large trader positions and position changes, large trader histories, and the potential for group trader activity. CFTC staff said that their economists keep their supervisors and the commission informed of potential problems as they arise.

CFTC Coordinates Its Surveillance and Oversight Activities with Others

In addition to keeping CFTC commissioners apprised of surveillance activities and specific cases that may require action, CFTC coordinates its surveillance and oversight activities with other federal agencies, states' attorneys general, and foreign regulators. CFTC officials told us that through the Division of Enforcement's Office of Cooperative Enforcement, which was created in 2002, they conduct outreach efforts to other financial regulators at the federal and state levels. Specifically, CFTC and FERC coordinate oversight and enforcement activities and have a memorandum of understanding that provides for the exchange of data. FERC regulates the interstate transmission of natural gas, oil, and electricity, and it audits natural gas sellers' compliance with the protocols outlined by FERC for reporting sales to index publishers like Platts, a company that compiles information on oil, natural gas, and electricity and other energy commodities and provides industry reports on commodity prices. If futures transactions are thought to affect transactions within FERC's jurisdiction, then FERC and CFTC may coordinate their oversight and enforcement work by sharing data as provided in the memorandum. In pursuing potential market abuse cases, such as individuals trying to manipulate energy spot prices to benefit their futures market positions, FERC officials said that FERC will tend to take the lead when abuses occur in the physical markets. FERC officials also said that CFTC will tend to take the lead when abuses occur in the futures markets. In July 2007, FERC filed two market manipulation cases that, according to a commission announcement, was the first time the agency used its enforcement authority under the Energy Policy Act of 2005 and its former market manipulation rule. According to CFTC officials, CFTC has filed 38 cases over the past 6 years that have focused on conduct in both the cash and futures markets (see app. IV). CFTC and FERC also may work with DOJ on certain cases.

In addition, CFTC officials said that, on occasion and when warranted by the circumstances, CFTC has shared large trader information with certain agencies, such as the Department of the Treasury, the Board of Governors of the Federal Reserve System, and the Federal Reserve Bank of New York, to address issues of common concern to the agencies. For example, in the aftermath of the financial difficulties in 1998 of Long Term Capital Management, a large hedge fund, CFTC shared information on the hedge fund's exchange trading activity with members of the President's Working Group. Because coordinating requires judgments about what information would need to be and could be shared and about how best to share it, we concluded in a 1999 report that the regulators are in the best position to determine the most effective ways to enhance their coordination.[59] CFTC also shares information with other members of the President's Corporate Fraud Task Force at their quarterly meetings on antifraud cases.

CFTC Energy-Related Enforcement Actions Generally Involved False Reporting and Attempted Manipulation, and Enforcement Actions Often Are Coordinated with Other Authorities

CFTC's Division of Enforcement is charged with enforcing the antimanipulation sections of the CEA, including sections 6(c), 6(d), and 9(a)(2). In particular, section 9(a)(2) sets forth the commission's antimanipulation and false reporting authority in cash and futures markets.[60] In determining whether violative conduct has occurred, CFTC officials told us that the Division of Enforcement has broad investigatory authority to obtain records and testimony, including subpoena authority, under a commission order. They added that upon conclusion of an investigation, which is routinely nonpublic, the division may recommend enforcement action if warranted.

The enforcement actions CFTC has taken in its energy-related cases generally have involved false public reporting as a method of attempting to manipulate prices on both the NYMEX futures market and the off-exchange markets. CFTC officials said that from October 2000 to September 2005, the commission initiated 287 enforcement cases and more than 30 of these cases involved energy trading, including actions against Enron and others. For example, according to CFTC data, from 2001 through 2005, CFTC levied fines totaling $305 million in actions alleging attempted manipulation of the price of natural gas (see app. IV for more detailed information). Most of these cases charged attempted manipulation by means of falsely reporting natural gas trading information to energy index firms, such as Platts, that calculate surveys or indexes of natural gas prices for various physical delivery points (hubs) throughout the United States. Generally, these cases involved allegations of various defendants knowingly disseminating false information in an effort to skew the indexes for their financial benefit or for other reasons. Participants in the natural gas markets use the indexes for price discovery and assessing price risk. Many of the actions were initiated on the basis of information that came from sources other than CFTC surveillance activities, or those of NYMEX, because they involved activities outside of NYMEX. As one major oil company official told us, in his view, CFTC and FERC vigorously pursued attempts by traders to manipulate the market.

Most recently, on August 1, 2007, the commission entered an order imposing a $1 million penalty against Marathon Petroleum Company, LLC, for attempting to manipulate spot cash crude prices by attempting to influence the Platts market assessment. On July 25, 2007, the commission commenced an action against Amaranth and others for attempted manipulation of NYMEX natural gas futures prices. Also on July 26, 2007, the commission commenced an enforcement action on Energy Transfer Partners, L.P., and others for attempted manipulation of physical natural gas prices.

Regarding energy futures, CFTC coordinates its enforcement activities with NYMEX officials and various other federal, state, and foreign authorities. CFTC staff stated that they meet periodically with NYMEX Compliance Department officials to discuss enforcement activities, as appropriate, and have formal quarterly meetings to discuss mutual involvement in specific cases, including energy products. In addition to coordinating energy enforcement matters with NYMEX, as a regulator of derivatives trading, CFTC often will work with the regulator of the underlying commodity or affected market, whether the Department of Agriculture, FERC, or Treasury. CFTC does not have criminal authority but often works with DOJ on those cases involving violations of the CEA that DOJ believes warrant criminal prosecution.[61] DOJ officials stated that their focus has been on natural gas cases, which began with cases involving Enron. According to DOJ officials, their role complemented the regulatory roles of FERC and CFTC, and they have an effective working relationship with CFTC in terms of sharing case information. For example, pursuant to a memorandum of understanding with CFTC, in May 2006, FERC obtained information about trading in natural gas futures contracts that FERC used in support of an enforcement action against Amaranth that was initiated in July 2007.[62] On July 25, 2007, CFTC filed an action in the United States District Court for the Southern District of New York against Amaranth Advisors, L.L.C., Amaranth Advisors (Calgary) ULC, and Brian Hunter alleging, among other things, that the defendants intentionally and unlawfully attempted to manipulate the price of natural gas futures contracts on NYMEX on February 24, 2006, and April 26, 2006.

In another case, on June 28, 2006, CFTC brought an enforcement action against BP Products North America, Inc., alleging, among other things, that BP cornered the physical propane market and manipulated the price of propane in February 2004.[63] Also on June 28, 2006, DOJ announced that a former BP trader had pled guilty to conspiracy to manipulate and corner the physical propane market. FTC also has exercised its authority in the energy arena. Since 1980, FTC's focus in energy has been in reviewing mergers and acquisitions for anticompetitive behavior and investigating instances of possible collusion, price fixing, and other anticompetitive conduct. However, FTC staff told us that they generally did not coordinate their work with CFTC, but added that they would turn over any evidence of futures manipulation to CFTC. CFTC staff said that, as appropriate, CFTC also coordinates its antifraud enforcement activities with states' attorneys general, who often will assist in a case by acting as a co-plaintiff with CFTC. In turn, CFTC may detail an attorney to a state. CFTC staff said that they also may work with international authorities, such as the United Kingdom's Financial Services Authority, on cases involving activities in more than one nation.

CFTC's Enforcement Program Received a Mixed OMB Rating but Lacks Effective Outcome-Based Performance Measures

Although CFTC has undertaken enforcement actions and levied fines, OMB's most recent 2004 Program Assessment Rating Tool (PART) assessment of the CFTC enforcement program was mixed. OMB designed PART to provide a consistent approach to assessing federal programs in the executive budget formulation process. PART is a standard series of questions meant to serve as a diagnostic performance tool, drawing on available program performance and evaluation information to form conclusions about program benefits and recommend adjustments that may improve results. In the assessment, OMB rated the enforcement program as "Results Not Demonstrated" and said that the enforcement program lacked performance measures that illustrate whether the program meets its overall objective. However, CFTC's existing performance measures show that it brings substantive cases in a timely manner and "is well designed to meet its objectives [of protecting commodity futures and options market users and the public from fraud, manipulation, and abusive practices related to the sale of certain commodities through the enforcement of laws against such practices] and to maximize the use of its resources." According to the PART assessment, the enforcement program has a clear purpose, addresses the public interest by ensuring adherence to the CEA and CFTC's regulations, is not duplicative of other government programs, is free of major design flaws, and is effectively targeted so that the resources address the program's purposes. OMB scored CFTC at 100 percent for the dimensions of both program purpose and design and program management, 71 percent for planning, and 67 percent for results and accountability. Compared with the other 96 programs that OMB identified as similar to CFTC's program, the comparable programs have much lower average scores for the dimensions of purpose and design (82 percent), program management (84 percent), and results and accountability (50 percent) and have a similar score for planning (73 percent).

CFTC's score of 71 percent for the planning dimension reflected OMB's assessment that CFTC included performance measures in its annual reports; used the actual results it achieved during the preceding fiscal year as a baseline for all of its performance measures and strove to set ambitious targets for its performance; was scrutinized on a regular basis by CFTC's Office of the Inspector General; had budget requests that were explicitly tied to accomplishment of the annual and long-term performance goals, and resource needs that were presented completely and transparently in the program's budget; and had taken meaningful steps to correct its strategic planning deficiencies. However, OMB also concluded that regarding the strategic planning dimension, the program had a limited number of long-term performance outcome measures that did not fully reflect the program's goals, and that the long-term measures and targets did not fully reflect the program's purposes. These measures included

- the percentage growth in market volume,
- the increase in the numbers of exchanges and clearinghouses,
- the percentages of SROs and clearing organizations that complied with the requirement to enforce their rules, and
- the percentage decreases in both the number of customers who lost funds because of alleged wrongdoing and the amount of funds that these customers lost.

CFTC enforcement staff stated that they face challenges in establishing measures to determine whether the enforcement program achieves its goal of deterring people from engaging in market manipulation or other abusive behavior.

According to OMB, CFTC's score of 67 percent on the program results and accountability dimension reflected its assessment that CFTC's enforcement program had demonstrated both (1) improved time efficiencies and cost-effectiveness in achieving its program goals and (2) our several evaluations of CFTC indicating that it was effective and achieving results.[64] OMB also reported that for fiscal year 2004, the enforcement program met all of its outcome measures and came close to meeting all of its output measures, with one exception. OMB further stated that the outcome-related measures established for enforcement do not fully reflect progress on meeting the program's overall goals.

While CFTC satisfied most but not all of OMB's PART criteria, it has fallen short in its ability to develop long-term performance outcome measures that are reflective of its program's goals and purposes. As OMB identified, CFTC has substituted proxy measures for outcome measures: that is, using measures such as percentage growth in market volume and increase in the number of exchanges and clearinghouses as proxies for protecting market integrity, and percentage decreases in both the number of customers who lost funds because of alleged wrongdoing as proxies for both protecting market integrity and consumers. We have found that managers in a regulatory environment where programs and activities are not easily measurable, as is the case with CFTC enforcement, have reported that it is particularly challenging to measure outcome-oriented performance and collect useful data.[65] However, there are a number of other ways to evaluate program effectiveness, such as using expert panel reviews, customer service surveys, and process and outcome evaluations. We have found with other programs that the form of the evaluations reflect differences in program structure and anticipated outcomes, and that the evaluations are designed around the programs and what they aim to achieve.[66] Without utilizing these or other methods to evaluate program effectiveness, CFTC is unable to demonstrate whether its enforcement program is meeting its overall objectives.

CONCLUSIONS

The rise in energy prices can be and has been attributed to a variety of factors. From January 2002 through June 2006, the physical and derivatives markets both underwent substantial change and evolution. The physical energy markets experienced tight supply and increasing global demand, ongoing political instability in oil-producing regions, and other supply disruptions, which affected the prices of energy products. At the same time, increasing numbers of and different types of market participants were trading futures in search of higher returns, thereby increasing contract volume. Substantial growth in the exempt commercial and OTC markets also occurred. Determining the impact of any one factor is complicated because price changes in the physical and futures markets are closely linked and in the long run are influenced by the same market fundamentals. Generally, futures prices reflect traders' views of the impact of changes in the physical markets and spot prices are affected by these expressed views and vice versa. Given this interrelationship, it is not surprising that some market observers point to the changes in the energy futures and other derivatives markets as a possible explanation for price increases, while others, primarily the regulators, look to changes in the physical markets to explain the increases. However, given the changes in both markets, attributing causality to any one factor—much less a particular type of trading activity—is difficult. Regardless of the reason for the increases in prices, ongoing monitoring of both markets is warranted to ensure that the public interest is being protected as well as the integrity of the markets.

Related to concerns about rising prices, some market observers and others have questioned whether CFTC's authority is broad enough to protect investors from fraudulent, manipulative, and abusive practices. The scope of CFTC's authority varies, depending on the market where the commodity is traded. Some markets are available for retail trading and receive direct CFTC oversight, while others are limited to professional traders (such as OTC energy derivatives markets) and receive less oversight. Other markets are largely unregulated. Given the changes in these markets in general and the growth in off-exchange trading in particular as well as ongoing questions about the relationship between exchange-traded and off-exchange markets, a reexamination of the scope of CFTC's authority is warranted. The results of CFTC's hearings on its existing regulatory structure and the similarities and differences between exchange-traded and exempt markets may be instructive for such a reexamination. While participants on all sides of this issue have perspectives that call for further consideration, these are public policy decisions that ultimately will be made by Congress. Unless resolved, questions will continue about the scope of CFTC's authority.

In the interim, we have identified a number of process issues that CFTC can address to strengthen its enforcement and surveillance programs.

- First, CFTC has attempted to provide the public with more meaningful information through the COT reports. While this effort has expanded the reporting for some agricultural commodities, it has remained virtually unchanged for energy commodities that have a high level of public and industry interest. Not having complete information on trading in energy commodities impairs the ability of traders to make fully informed decisions.

- Second, CFTC's oversight of regulated exchanges involves a range of surveillance activities that have resulted in a number of commission-related enforcement actions. However, CFTC does not maintain complete records of its surveillance activities. Currently, the commission does not maintain written records on all surveillance follow-up activities, particularly in instances where no potential violation was found. Without such records, CFTC staff cannot fully demonstrate the actions they are taking to combat fraud and manipulation in the markets.

- Third, as is the case with most enforcement agencies, CFTC has had limited success in identifying meaningful outcome-based performance measures. However, agencies can use a variety of methods to evaluate program effectiveness, such as expert panel reviews, customer service surveys, and process and outcome evaluations. Without meaningful measures for program effectiveness, CFTC may be missing opportunities to identify significant trends in certain activities or markets and to better target its limited resources.

MATTER FOR CONGRESSIONAL CONSIDERATION

In light of recent developments in derivatives markets and as part of CFTC's reauthorization process, Congress should consider further exploring whether the current regulatory structure for energy derivatives, in particular for those traded in exempt commercial markets, provides adequately for fair trading and accurate pricing of energy commodities.

RECOMMENDATIONS FOR EXECUTIVE ACTION

To improve the oversight and available information on energy futures trading, we recommend that the Acting CFTC Chairman take the following three actions:

- reexamine the classifications in the COT reports to determine if the commercial and noncommercial trading categories should be refined to improve the accuracy and relevance of public information provided to the energy futures markets;
- explore ways to routinely maintain written records of inquiries into possible improper trading activity and the results of these inquiries to more fully determine the usefulness and extent of CFTC's surveillance, antifraud, and antimanipulation authorities; and
- examine ways to more fully demonstrate the effectiveness of CFTC enforcement activities by developing additional outcome-related performance measures that more fully reflect progress in meeting the program's overall goals.

AGENCY COMMENTS

We provided a draft of this report to the Commodity Futures Trading Commission for comment. In its written comments, CFTC said that the commission will reexamine classifications in the COT reports. CFTC also said that the commission will explore additional recordkeeping procedures for its staff, but that it must balance the time required for such additional tasks against the need to undertake market surveillance by an already-stretched surveillance staff. CFTC added that it has included the development of measures to evaluate the effectiveness of its enforcement program in its most recent strategic plan.

Orice M. Williams
Director, Financial Markets and
Community Investment

List of Congressional Addressees

The Honorable Tom Harkin
Chairman
The Honorable Saxby Chambliss
Ranking Member Committee on Agriculture, Nutrition and Forestry
United States Senate

The Honorable Jeff Bingaman
Chairman
The Honorable Pete V. Domenici
Ranking Member
Committee on Energy and Natural Resources
United States Senate

The Honorable Carl Levin
Chairman
The Honorable Norm Coleman
Ranking Member
Permanent Subcommittee on Investigations Committee on
Homeland Security and Governmental Affairs
United States Senate
The Honorable Collin C. Peterson
Chairman
The Honorable Bob Goodlatte
Ranking Republican Member
Committee on Agriculture
House of Representatives

The Honorable John Dingell
Chairman
The Honorable Joe Barton
Ranking Member
Committee on Energy and Commerce
House of Representatives

The Honorable Henry A. Waxman
Chairman
The Honorable Tom Davis

Ranking Member
Committee on Oversight and Government Reform
House of Representatives

The Honorable Bob Etheridge
Chairman
The Honorable Jerry Moran
Ranking Member
Subcommittee on General Farm Commodities and Risk Management
Committee on Agriculture
House of Representatives

The Honorable Maria Cantwell
United States Senate

The Honorable Norm Coleman
United States Senate

The Honorable Daniel Inouye
United States Senate

The Honorable Robert Menendez
United States Senate

The Honorable Ben Nelson
United States Senate

The Honorable Olympia Snowe
United States Senate

The Honorable Robert Andrews
House of Representatives

The Honorable Tammy Baldwin
House of Representatives

The Honorable Jim Cooper
House of Representatives

The Honorable Peter DeFazio
House of Representatives

The Honorable John J. Duncan, Jr.
House of Representatives

The Honorable Scott Garrett
House of Representatives

The Honorable Doc Hastings
House of Representatives

The Honorable Mike Honda
House of Representatives
The Honorable Darlene Hooley
House of Representatives

The Honorable Dale Kildee
House of Representatives

The Honorable John Larson
House of Representatives

The Honorable Bill Pascrell, Jr.
House of Representatives

The Honorable Cathy McMorris Rodgers
House of Representatives

The Honorable Mike Rogers (MI)
House of Representatives

The Honorable Steven Rothman
House of Representatives

The Honorable Lucille Roybal-Allard
House of Representatives

The Honorable Mike Simpson
House of Representatives

The Honorable Adam Smith
House of Representatives

The Honorable Greg Walden
House of Representatives

APPENDIX I: SCOPE AND METHODOLOGY

To examine trends and patterns of trading activity in the energy derivatives markets and physical markets, we analyzed data on futures, spot, and over-the-counter (OTC) derivative markets. We gathered information on spot prices for crude oil, unleaded gasoline, heating oil, and natural gas from the U.S. Department of Energy's Energy Information Administration (EIA). We obtained daily futures settlement prices and average daily volume data for the four commodities from the New York Mercantile Exchange, Inc. (NYMEX). We collected data on the size of the global OTC commodity derivatives market—including energy, but excluding precious metals—from the Bank for International Settlements. We also obtained information on the numbers of participants and outstanding positions in energy futures markets by different categories of traders from the Commodity Futures Trading Commission (CFTC). These CFTC data cover the period from July 2003 through December 2006. We determined that data from these sources were sufficiently reliable for the purposes of this report.

We used monthly averages of the EIA spot prices and NYMEX futures prices to depict price trends over the past 20 years and illustrate the strong relationship between spot and futures prices. Also, we adjusted the prices to remove the effects of inflation so that prices would be comparable across years. We also adjusted the prices using monthly deflation factors that we derived from the seasonally adjusted implicit price deflator for gross domestic product from the Bureau of Economic Analysis, as of February 28, 2007.

We used the futures price data obtained from NYMEX to calculate the volatility of energy futures prices. These data covered the period from January 1987 through December 2006 for crude oil, unleaded gasoline, and heating oil. The period for natural gas was from April 1990 through December 2006, when that contract began trading on NYMEX. We calculated the historical volatility of the futures prices as the standard deviation of the natural logarithm of relative changes in daily settlement prices. Monthly volatility figures were calculated from the trading days of each month and expressed on an annual basis. We annualized the monthly figures by multiplying daily volatility by the square root of 250, which represents an approximation of the number of trading days in a year. We also calculated annual volatility for each of the four commodities as the average of the monthly mean volatilities. We used the front month futures contract—that is, the nearest traded contract month—because it is the most frequently used maturity for measuring price and volatility and is the most heavily traded contract.

To identify the opinions of market participants and analysts about the effect of energy derivatives trading on prices, we interviewed officials from CFTC, the Federal Energy Regulatory Commission, and EIA; managers from trading facilities, including NYMEX and the IntercontinentalExchange (ICE); academics knowledgeable about energy and finance; and market participants representing investment banks, hedge funds, and oil producers and refiners. We selected banks to interview on the basis of their perceived level of involvement in energy markets. The hedge funds we interviewed were identified through the assistance of the Managed Funds Association—a membership organization representing the hedge fund industry—which contacted its members involved in energy trading to identify hedge funds who were willing to be interviewed. We selected oil producers and refiners on the basis of their size and role in U.S. energy markets. We also gathered information from several trade associations, including those representing users of energy commodities, and interviewed former CFTC officials. Although we gathered the views of a wide range of market participants and observers, these sources do not necessarily represent the views of all market participants and observers. We also reviewed studies by governmental and nongovernmental observers, including CFTC; NYMEX; the Senate's Permanent Subcommittee on Investigations, Committee on Homeland Security and Governmental Affairs; and a report prepared for the attorneys general of four midwestern states. In addition, we reviewed public statements from relevant government officials, such as the current Federal Reserve chairman and his predecessor. To understand the effects of supply and demand conditions in the physical energy markets, we examined data and analysis from EIA and prior GAO reports.

To examine CFTC's resources and authority for protecting market users from fraudulent, manipulative, and abusive practices in the trading of energy futures contracts, we describe CFTC's current and past regulatory authority and approach by reviewing the Commodity Exchange Act (CEA), as amended; CFTC's President's Budget and Performance Plan for fiscal year 2007; CFTC's 2004 Annual Report; and other information from CFTC. We obtained information on CFTC's regulatory role and the exempt commercial and OTC markets from officials at CFTC, EIA, and NYMEX and from market participants. In addition, we reviewed information on CFTC's regulatory role contained in the *Federal Register* and congressional hearing testimony. To describe the concerns regarding OTC derivative trading and the scope of CFTC's regulatory authority, we obtained information from federal agency officials and an industry trade association. To describe the hedging and speculative trading of market participants, we reviewed various reports that addressed those concerns, and we interviewed several market participants.

To examine how CFTC monitors and detects market abuses in the trading of energy futures, and enforcement actions taken in response to identified abuses, we gathered information from officials at CFTC headquarters and the New York Regional Office. We reviewed CFTC regulations and other documents on its surveillance and enforcement programs and observed a CFTC monthly surveillance meeting. We gathered information from market participants and experts regarding CFTC's oversight activities. To examine CFTC's enforcement program and how CFTC coordinates with other regulators and authorities, we gathered and analyzed data on CFTC's enforcement cases, interviewed CFTC and other federal agency officials and staff on coordination activities and agreements, and reviewed CFTC Office of the Inspector General reports. We also reviewed the Office of Management and Budget's PART assessment of CFTC's enforcement program.

APPENDIX II: TYPES OF CONTRACTS AND TRANSACTIONS FOR ENERGY COMMODITIES IN THE PHYSICAL AND FINANCIAL MARKETS

Markets	Type of contract or transaction	Features
Physical	Spot	Bilateral over-the-counter (OTC) transactions for immediate delivery or near-term delivery and payment representing a specific price and location. Industry analysts publish price data gathered from market participants.
	Forward	Bilateral OTC transactions in which the seller agrees to deliver to the buyer a specified quantity and quality of an asset or a commodity at a specified date at an agreed-upon

		price or pricing formula and where delivery is contemplated.
Financial	Derivatives traded on U.S. regulated exchanges	Futures contracts are standardized contracts for a specific product at a specific location, where delivery is not usually made and contracts are offset prior to expiration. Tran-sactions are executed on an exchange regulated by the Commodity Futures Trading Commission (CFTC), such as the New York Mercantile Exchange. The exchange publicly disseminates price and other data. Options on futures contracts are contracts that give a buy-er the right, but not the obligation, to buy or sell a specific quantity of futures contracts within a designated period at a designated price.
	Derivatives traded on foreign boards of trade subject to foreign regulation	As in the United States, standardized contracts for a specific product at a specific location, where delivery is not usually made and contracts are usually offset prior to expiration. Sales are executed on an exchange, such as the IntercontinentalExchange (ICE) Futures in London that is subject to regulation by the U.K. Financial Services Authority. Foreign boards of trade are able to provide direct access to U.S. market participants by obtaining "no-action" relief from CFTC staff.
	Derivatives traded on exempt commercial markets	Standardized contracts for a specific product at a specific location, where delivery is not usually contemplated because contracts are usually offset prior to expiration or are cash settled and are based on prices from a regulated futu-res exchange or another source. Transactions are executed on an electronic trading platform, such as ICE, involving "eligible commercial entities." Exempt commercial markets may offer a clearing service for certain derivatives contracts. Exempt commercial markets may offer trading both in contracts that are subject to the Commodity Exchange Act and contracts that are not.
	Bilateral OTC derivatives	Derivatives contracts that are privately negotiated, bilate-ral contracts between eligible counter parties, often involving a swap dealer. The contracts are financially settled and are based on prices from a regulated futures exchange or another source. OTC swaps are a promise between two parties to make a series of payments to each other, of which at least one series is based on a commodity price. OTC options: OTC markets also offer options to buy or sell other assets.

Sources: CFTC and GAO.

Note: Forward contracts have characteristics that make them similar to futures derivative contracts traded in a financial market. Both contracts represent agreements in which one party agrees to purchase a specified amount of an economic good at a specified price from another party at a future date or during some future period. For the purposes of this table, we chose to place forward contracts in the physical market category, rather than the financial market category, because parties entering into forward contracts are more likely to have the intention of exchanging the commodity than are parties entering into futures contracts. Parties entering into derivatives contracts rarely carry out an exchange of the physical commodity, as their purpose in entering the transaction is to assume or offset price risk.

APPENDIX III: NEW YORK MERCANTILE EXCHANGE SURVEILLANCE AND ENFORCEMENT ACTIVITIES

NYMEX Conducts Surveillance of Both Market and Trading Activities

Under CFTC regulations, NYMEX is responsible for establishing and enforcing rules governing its member conduct and trading, preventing market manipulation, ensuring that futures industry professionals meet qualifications, and examining members for financial strength. In carrying out these responsibilities, NYMEX officials told us that NYMEX's surveillance program is designed to monitor market and trade practices. They said that NYMEX relies on automated detailed information for each transaction to identify the buyer, seller, and clearing members who maintain customer accounts, and to identify whether a person is a member of NYMEX. The market surveillance activities focus on monitoring for possible manipulation by market participants. Specifically, NYMEX officials monitor large trader data, the "street book" speculative position limits and accountability levels, exemptions to speculative position limits, position concentrations, and the relationship between cash and futures prices.[67] A speculative position limit is the maximum net position that a market participant may hold in a specified contract month of a listed NYMEX contract, and is set by NYMEX. Market participants that are bona fide hedgers are eligible to apply for, and receive under certain conditions, limited exemptions from speculative position limits.

NYMEX officials said that they monitor speculative position limits, and if a limit is about to be reached or has been hit, they record the overage and contact the customer to find out if there is a logical explanation for the overage that is linked to a bona fide commercial exposure. They added that if there is a logical explanation, the customer may be allowed to keep the position and file for a formal exemption; however, if there is no logical explanation, then NYMEX officials will direct the position to be reduced. The officials said they follow such directives with a warning letter to the customer. If the position is not reduced, the officials said that another warning letter is then to be issued. As a final step, NYMEX could hold a hearing before its business conduct committee to deny the customer access to the exchange. However, this has never happened, according to NYMEX officials. They also said that customers may obtain exemptions to speculative position limits on a case-by-case basis and for a period of 12 months. The officials said that exemptions are not given if they could disrupt the markets, and that the exemptions are monitored for possible changing circumstances, such as reorganizations or Moody's downgrading a party's equity rating.

NYMEX also monitors trading by customers using multiple brokers. For example, NYMEX officials stated that large oil companies may use several brokers to trade—that is, each broker may trade using its own account to hide what it is doing from other companies. However, NYMEX officials said that all of the company's accounts are aggregated, and that its staff will analyze the trading and large trader data and contact the customer if there are any surveillance issues. In addition, NYMEX has established the maximum daily trading limits for each commodity contract. These limits are the maximum price advance or decline from the prior day's settlement price and, if exceeded, trading stops for a period. NYMEX officials said that the exchange has changed these limits over the years, and the officials could not recall the last time a trading limit was reached. Furthermore, the limits were completely eliminated for NYMEX's New York Commodity Exchange (COMEX) division, which trades precious metals. According to NYMEX officials, suspending trading would give traders time to count and balance their positions before resuming trading. Unfortunately, the officials continued, if trading on NYMEX is suspended, the price discovery mechanism on which the OTC and cash markets depend is also suspended. They added that CFTC does not provide any requirements for price limits and, in fact, favors ongoing price discovery.

In addition to market surveillance, NYMEX conducts trade practice surveillance. According to NYMEX officials, this surveillance focuses on persons who handle contract orders either on the trading floor or electronically, as well as on persons and firms engaging in proprietary trading for their own accounts. NYMEX seeks to identify trading practice abuses, such as prearranged trading, front running, providing tips on proprietary information, and accommodating trades. Prearranged trading is the noncompetitive trading between brokers in accordance with an expressed or implied agreement or understanding and is a violation of CEA and CFTC regulations. Front running is taking a futures or option position based on, for example, a customer order in the same or related future or option. This practice is also known as trading ahead. Accommodation trading is noncompetitive trading entered into by a trader, usually to assist another with illegal trades. NYMEX officials stated that trade practice surveillance information may be used as part of market surveillance, but this surveillance is not as focused on price movements and involves different types of monitoring, such as physically observing floor trading by people entering orders, and, in effect, is similar to "police on the beat." The officials added that with their recent use of the Chicago Mercantile Exchange's Globex electronic trading system to trade energy futures, their trade practice surveillance system is changing, with more emphasis on monitoring access to, and activity on, the Globex system in NYMEX contracts.

NYMEX Uses Information from Surveillance Activities and Other Sources for Enforcement Cases

As a self-regulatory organization (SRO), NYMEX has the authority to pursue instances of suspected manipulation or other attempts of fraudulent or abusive trading. NYMEX officials stated that the exchange conducts its own enforcement activities, and CFTC expects NYMEX as an SRO to handle issues relating to exchange members. However, NYMEX will request CFTC's assistance if needed, especially for issues relating to nonexchange members. If NYMEX officials become aware of potentially abusive practices outside of their authority, they will notify the appropriate federal regulator, such as CFTC. Information from NYMEX surveillance activities and other sources is used to investigate potential abuses. Other sources of information include referrals from CFTC, traders, and customers. NYMEX officials investigate these referrals; if there is evidence of wrongdoing, they may open an investigation case. For each case that is pursued, they record information, including the source of the referral and investigation activities. Interviews conducted during an investigation may be taped and transcribed. From January 2000 through May 2006, NYMEX opened 706 investigations. However, if a referral did not result in a case that was pursued, NYMEX does not document how each referral was handled. For example, if a referral regarding a trade resulted in a NYMEX official making a telephone call and finding that there was no apparent violation, NYMEX officials said staff would not create a written record to log how the referral was handled or the result of the inquiry.

NYMEX officials told us that when NYMEX pursues a case, such as prearranged trading, the case is brought before the exchange's business conduct committee (BCC).[68] According to NYMEX, the BCC (which includes three public members and other committee members), is structured in a manner analogous to a grand jury proceeding and determines, on the basis of the evidence in an investigative report and any written response from the person accused in the case, whether there is a reasonable basis to believe an exchange rule violation occurred. NYMEX officials told us that a BCC meeting is scheduled for every other month; however, in some months, there are no cases to discuss and no meetings are held. They added that the BCC hears about two or three dozen cases annually. Once a case is heard, the BCC may then direct the compliance department to issue a complaint, or, in the case of minor violations, a written warning. The person named in the complaint has 10 days to respond, and he or she may make a settlement offer at any time prior to the conclusion of a hearing. Settlement offers must be approved by NYMEX's board of directors. From January 2000 through May 2006, NYMEX opened more than 700 investigations, most involving trading violations, and, of those, 125 were BCC-issued complaints (see table 2).[69]

Settlement of NYMEX complaints may result in settlement offers, fines, or disciplinary actions. Settlement offers exceeding $25,000, or cases contested by the respondent, are referred to NYMEX's adjudication committee for settlement consideration or for a full disciplinary hearing. The adjudication committee is authorized to conduct hearings where the facts of the case are presented and argued by the respondent or their attorney and exchange compliance counsel. At the conclusion of the hearing, the committee issues a decision regarding any sanctions. Sanctions can include a cease-and-desist order, a fine of up to $250,000 for each rule violation, suspension, or expulsion from membership. For example, NYMEX settled a $100,000 case on Morgan Stanley in 2002, a $2.5 million case on BP Product North America, Inc., in 2003, and a $300,000 case on Shell in 2005. NYMEX officials stated that no one has been expelled from the exchange since 1998 for failure to pay a fine. According to the officials, the adjudication committee is scheduled to meet at least once a month. They added that about 40 percent of the cases are resolved at adjudication and cases rarely go to a full hearing. If a hearing does occur, the decisions can be appealed to NYMEX's appeals committee, which makes a final determination within the exchange. Cases then can be appealed further to CFTC, but cases involving an appeal of an exchange appeals committee decision rarely are contested or proceed to a hearing. NYMEX officials said that the commission rarely, if ever, overturns a NYMEX ruling. NYMEX publishes its final disciplinary actions of the exchange. All settlements or adjudications are published in its monthly publication *The Open Interest* (formerly, *Barrels, Bars and BTUs*) and sent to the National Futures Association, where they are included in the publicly accessible disciplinary log called "BASIC," which contains reports from all U.S. futures exchanges and from CFTC. Warning letters are not reported, but they are used internally in prosecuting disciplinary cases. NYMEX also reports its enforcement actions to CFTC.

Table 2. Number of NYMEX Enforcement Cases Opened, Complaints Issued, Settlement, and Hearings, January 2000–May 2006

Year	Number of investigations opened[a]	Number of complaints issued[b]	Number of respondents[c]	Number settled at BCC[d]	Number settled at Adjudication[e]	Number contested at hearings and adjudication[f]	Hearing results[g]
2000	101	19	21	4	13	2	Dismissed. Charges affirmed on appeal; fine and suspension reduced.[b]
2001	88	21	28	3	22	0	
2002	115	21	27	9	16	0	
2003	123	16	22	9	14	1	Rule violations found; fine.
2004	111	18	28	11	11	0	
2005	97	24	37	3	23	1	Decision pending.
2006	71	6	9	2	4	0	

Source: GAO analysis of NYMEX data.

Note: The number of complaints and respondents do not correspond to the settled and hearing numbers on a one-for-one basis.

[a] Number of investigations opened is based on investigations opened within the calendar years 2000, 2001, 2002, 2003, 2004, 2005 and through May 2006 (and taken from an annual review of the Compliance Department conducted by NYMEX's legal staff for a report to the Board). Not all inquiries become formal investigations. For instance, in 2005, the market surveillance area reported 887 "cases" on their rule violation and e-inquiry log. The vast majority of these were routine position limit reviews, exchange for physical and exchange of futures for swaps inquiries, and unreported reviews that never became formal investigations. The trade practice area logs "inquires," which may or may not evolve into formal investigations.

[b] Number of complaints issued represents the number of complaints issued by the BCC during the year specified, but only for investigations opened in one of the target years (2000 through May 2006).

c Number of respondents represents the number of individuals charged in the various BCC cases.

d Number settled at BCC represents the number of individuals who settled cases from a target year before the BCC.

e Number settled at adjudication represents the number of individuals who settled cases from a target year before the adjudication committee, which has authority similar to a judge and jury.

f Number contested at hearings and adjudication indicates any cases that were contested (rather than settled) and proceeded to a hearing or adjudication.

g Hearing results also encompass the results of adjudications.

To maintain its designation as a contract market, NYMEX must demonstrate to CFTC its capacity to comply with the CEA's core principles. In addition, CFTC conducts rule enforcement reviews and publicly reports on how NYMEX exercises its enforcement authority and other areas of operations. In 2004, CFTC reported that NYMEX's disciplinary program provided reasonable sanctions for a majority of the cases where the exchange took disciplinary action, and that its dispute resolution program had fair and equitable procedures. The report was generally positive and reported that NYMEX's procedures provided for the recording and safe storage of trade information. Furthermore, NYMEX's surveillance of trade practices was deemed to be adequate, with thorough and well-documented investigations. NYMEX officials told us that a CFTC rule enforcement review was recently initiated at the exchange.

APPENDIX IV: COMMODITY FUTURES TRADING COMMISSION'S ENERGY-RELATED ENFORCEMENT ACTIONS, AUGUST 2001 - SEPTEMBER 2006

Table 3 reflects information obtained from CFTC showing the energy-related enforcement actions it took by CFTC from August 2001 through September 2006. The enforcement cases were against individuals and companies, and the information used to initiate the investigation originated from both within CFTC and from outside of the commission. The actions mostly focused on attempts to manipulate energy commodity prices through alleged attempts of false reporting; some also involved alleged wash sales or trades—transactions intended to give the appearance that purchases and sales have been made, without incurring market risk or changing the trader's market position, prearranged trading, and recordkeeping violations. CFTC's information also shows a wide range of civil monetary penalties.

Table 3. Energy-Related Enforcement Actions Filed by CFTC, August 2001–September 2006

Date case filed	CFTC enforcement case	Initial source of information CFTC used to initiate the investigation (CFTC/ external/individual)	Reason for charges	Civil monetary penalties
09/2006	Dominion Resources, Inc.	CFTC	False reporting	$4.3 million
06/2006	BP Products North America, Inc.	External	Manipulation, cornering the market, and attempted mani-pulation	In litigation
01/2006	Shell Trading US Company and Shell International Trading and Shipping Co., Nigel Catterall	External	Prearranged trading	$300,000
09/2005	Joseph Foley	CFTC/External	Attempted manipulation and false reporting	$350,000
05/2005	Brion Scott McKenna	CFTC	Manipulation	Registration revoked
04/2005	Andrew Richmond	CFTC/External	Attempted manipulation and false reporting	$60,000
02/2005	Christopher McDonald, Michael Whalen, and Paul Atha	CFTC/External	Attempted manipulation and false reporting	$350,000 $200,000 In litigation
02/2005	Matthew Reed, Darrell Danyluk, Shawn Mclaughlin, and	CFTC	Attempted manipulation and false reporting	In litigation $350,000 $450,000 $800,000

	Concord Energy			
02/2005	Jeffrey A. Bradley, Robert Martin	External	Attempted manipulation and false reporting	In litigation In litigation
02/2005	Denette Johnson, Courtney Cubbison Moore, John Tracy, Robert Harp, Anthony Dizona, and Kelly Dyer	External	Attempted manipulation and false reporting	All in litigation
02/2005	Michael Whitney	External	Attempted manipulation and false reporting	In litigation
12/2004	Mirant Americas Energy Marketing, L.P.	CFTC/External	Attempted manipulation and false reporting	$12.5 million
11/2004	Cinergy Marketing and Trading, L.P.	CFTC/External	False reporting	$3 million
11/2004	BP Energy Company	CFTC	Wash trades	$100,000
08/2004	Byron Biggs	CFTC	Wash trades	$30,000
07/2004	United Energy and Dana Christopher Bray	CFTC/External	Recordkeeping violations	$33,000
07/2004	NRG Energy, Inc.	CFTC	False reporting	$2 million
07/2004	Coral Energy Resources, L.P.	External	Attempted manipulation and false reporting	$30 million
07/2004	Western Gas Resources	CFTC/External	Attempted manipulation and false reporting	$7 million
01/2004	Robert Benjamin Harmon, Jr.	External	Wash trades	$7,500
05/2004	Joseph Knauth	CFTC	Wash trades	$25,000

Table 3. (Continued)

Date case filed	CFTC enforcement case	Initial source of information CFTC used to initiate the investigation (CFTC/ external/individual)	Reason for charges	Civil monetary penalties
05/2004	Enron Corporation and Hunter S. Shively	CFTC/External	Manipulation or attempted manipulation. Enron only: Operating illegal futures exchange and trading an off-exchange agricultural futures contract	$35 million $300,000
01/2004	Calpine Corporation	CFTC	False reporting	$1.5 million
01/2004	ONEOK, Inc., ONEOK Energy Marketing and Trading Co., L.P.	Individual	False reporting	$3 million
01/2004	Entergy Koch Trading L.P.	External	False reporting	$3 million
01/2004	e prime	CFTC/External	Attempted manipulation and false reporting	$16 million
01/2004	Aquila Merchant Services	CFTC/External	Attempted manipulation and false reporting	$26.5 million
11/2003	CMS Marketing Services and Trading; CMS Field Services	External	Attempted manipulation and false reporting	$16 million
11/2003	Reliant Energy Services, Inc.	External	Attempted manipulation and false reporting, and wash sales	$18 million
09/2003	William Taylor	CFTC	Attempted Manipulation	$155,000
09/2003	Michael Garber, NYMEX floor broker	External	Wash sales, reported non-bona fide prices, and noncompetitive trading	$7,500

09/2003	American Electric Power Company (AEP) and AEP Energy Services (AEPES)	CFTC/External	Attempted manipulation and false reporting	$30 million
09/2003	Duke Energy Trading and Marketing, L.L.C.	External	Attempted manipulation and false reporting	$28 million
07/2003	Enserco Energy	CFTC	Attempted manipulation and false reporting	$3 million
07/2003	Williams Companies and Williams Energy Marketing and Trading	CFTC/External	Attempted manipulation and false reporting	$20 million
07/2003	W. D. Energy Services, Inc. (Encana)	External	Attempted manipulation and false reporting	$20 million
03/2003	Christopher Chapman	External	Fraudulent trading	$240,000
03/2003	El Paso Merchant Energy	CFTC/External	Attempted manipulation and false reporting	$20 million
12/2002	Dynegy Marketing and Trade and West Coast Power	CFTC	Attempted manipulation and false reporting	$5 million
08/2001	Robert Kristufek	CFTC	Attempted manipulation	$155,000
08/2001	Thomas Johns, Michael Griswold, and Avista Energy	CFTC	Attempted manipulation	$50,000 $110,000 $2.1 million

Source: CFTC.

Note: According to CFTC, AEPES entered into a deferred prosecution agreement with the Department of Justice and the U.S. Attorney's Office for the Southern District of Ohio to avoid federal criminal charges. The agreement requires AEPES to pay a $30 million criminal penalty to resolve an investigation into AEPES' false reporting of natural gas trades. In addition, AEP accepted a settlement agreement with the Federal Energy Regulatory Commission (FERC) to resolve an investigation into the natural gas storage and transportation activities of two intrastate pipeline units formerly owned by AEP and AEP-affiliated marketers. The FERC settlement requires AEP to pay a $21 million civil penalty and adopt a compliance plan to prevent future violations. The total settlement with the U.S. government was $81 million.

APPENDIX V: COMMENTS FROM THE COMMODITY FUTURES TRADING COMMISSION

U.S. Commodity Futures Trading Commission
Three Lafayette Centre,1155 21st Street, NW, Washington, DC 20581

Walter L. Lukken
Acting Chairman

(202) 418-5014
(202) 418-5550 Facsimile
wlukken@cftc.gov

October 5, 2007

Orice M. Williams
Director
Financial Markets and Community Investment
U.S. General Accountability Office
441 G Street, NW
Washington, DC 20548

Dear Ms. Williams:

Thank you for all of the time, attention, and effort that GAO has devoted to understanding the nation's energy futures markets and reviewing the oversight of those markets by the Commodity Futures Trading Commission (CFTC or Commission). We are pleased that the GAO recognized the Commission's vigorous oversight of the regulated futures markets. This letter responds to specific GAO recommendations for improved information, recordkeeping, and evaluations below.

In this report, GAO suggested one matter for Congressional consideration. GAO stated that "[i]n light of recent developments in derivatives markets and as part of CFTC's reauthorization process, Congress should further explore whether the current regulatory structure for energy derivatives, in particular for those traded in exempt commercial markets, provides adequately for fair trading and accurate pricing of energy commodities."

The appropriate regulatory structure for energy derivatives has been a matter of consideration for the Congress, the courts, and the CFTC at various times during the past twenty years as the industry and the role it plays in the nation's economy has evolved. This matter is currently of great interest to the Commission, which held a public hearing on September 18, 2007 to examine the oversight of trading on regulated futures exchanges and Exempt Commercial Markets (ECMs). Witnesses included members of the energy trading community, financial services trade associations, and energy consumer groups. The Commission anticipates providing Congress with recommendations in the near future to help inform the debate.

GAO also recommends that the Chairman of the CFTC take three actions to improve oversight and available information of energy futures trading.

1. Re-examine classifications in the COT reports to determine whether the commercial and non-commercial trading categories should be refined to improve the accuracy and relevance of public information provided in the energy futures markets.

As discussed in the report, the Commission is publishing additional information about commodity index traders in certain agricultural commodities traded on Designated Contract Markets. As part of that decision, the staff examined the possibility of similarly expanding the information available about energy and metals trading. The staff found that in the case of energy and metals markets, however, there are alternative U.S. and non-U.S. exchanges and a multitude of OTC markets and derivative products. Many swap dealers, in addition to their commodity index-related OTC activity, enter into other OTC derivative transactions in individual commodities, both with commercial firms hedging price risk and with speculators taking on price risk. In addition, some swap dealers are very actively engaged in commercial activity in the underlying cash market, such as a physical merchandising or dealing activity. As a result of these other activities, the overall futures positions held by these energy and metals traders in Commission-regulated markets do not necessarily correspond closely with their hedging of OTC commodity index transactions. It would be difficult, if not impossible, to link these residual futures positions with any particular part of the underlying activity that makes up the "book" of the swap dealer. At that time, the Commission concluded that including the energy and metal markets in supplemental COT information would seriously mislead the public as to the actual amount of index trading and the amount of commercial trading that was present in those markets.

Nevertheless, the Commission will re-examine classifications in the COT reports to determine whether the COT reports should be refined to improve accuracy and relevance of public information about energy futures markets.

2. Explore ways to routinely maintain written records of inquiries to more fully determine the usefulness and extent of its surveillance, anti-fraud, and anti-manipulation authorities.

As the report makes clear, the written records of surveillance inquiries that are further pursued are adequately documented. However, GAO has recommended documenting the decision not to further pursue surveillance inquiries – something that is not currently done. The Commission agrees further documentation of decisions about surveillance inquiries could assist the Commission in the management of its staff resources and could be beneficial to Congressional oversight. Accordingly, the Commission will explore additional record keeping procedures for staff, but must balance the time required for such additional tasks against the need to undertake market surveillance by an already-stretched surveillance staff.

3. Examine ways to more fully demonstrate effectiveness of its enforcement activities by developing additional outcome-related performance measures that more fully reflect progress on meeting the program's overall goals.

Enforcement agencies generally have great difficulty demonstrating their effectiveness. In short, it is easy to measure actions, such as cases brought, cases won, and penalties imposed, but it is very difficult to measure prevented actions – that is, how many violations of the law have been deterred. Nevertheless, the Commission, like other law enforcement agencies, wishes to improve effectiveness in this area. The Commission agrees with the GAO that this matter should be examined and has included in the Commission's most recent Strategic Plan the development of measures to evaluate the effectiveness of the Commission's enforcement efforts.

To that end, the Commission had requested in the past, and will continue to request, funding to study the feasibility of developing measures that better reflect program effectiveness including:

* developing novel ways of measuring results, for instance surveying industry experts, investigating methodologies for determining non-compliance,
* developing measures that quantify increased efficiencies, and
* developing measures and targets for the collection of fines.

We have been unsuccessful to date securing funding for this project but we will continue to seek resources for the expertise needed to undertake this project.

Again, I want to thank you and your staff for their work on this project and look forward to working with you on your next study involving the CFTC.

Sincerely,

Related GAO Products

Energy Markets: Factors Contributing to Higher Gasoline Prices. GAO-06-412T. Washington, D.C.: February 1, 2006.

Natural Gas and Electricity Markets: Federal Government Actions to Improve Private Price Indices and Stakeholder Reaction. GAO-06-275. Washington, D.C.: December 15, 2005.

SEC and CFTC Penalties: Continued Progress Made in Collection Efforts, but Greater SEC Management Attention Is Needed. GAO-05-670. Washington, D.C.: August 31, 2005.

Mutual Fund Industry: SEC's Revised Examination Approach Offers Potential Benefits, but Significant Oversight Challenges Remain. GAO-05-415. Washington, D.C.: August 17, 2005.

National Energy Policy: Inventory of Major Federal Energy Programs and Status of Policy Recommendations. GAO-05-379. Washington, D.C.: June 10, 2005.

Motor Fuels: Understanding the Factors That Influence the Retail Price of Gasoline. GAO-05-525SP. Washington, D.C.: May 2005.

Mutual Fund Trading Abuses: SEC Consistently Applied Procedures in Setting Penalties, but Could Strengthen Certain Internal Controls. GAO-05-385. Washington, D.C.: May 16, 2005.

Financial Regulation: Industry Changes Prompt Need to Reconsider U.S. Regulatory Structure. GAO-05-61. Washington, D.C.: October 6, 2004.

Natural Gas: Domestic Nitrogen Fertilizer Production Depends on Natural Gas Availability and Prices. GAO-03-1148. Washington, D.C.: September 30, 2003.

SEC and CFTC Fines Follow-up: Collection Programs Are Improving, but Further Steps Are Warranted. GAO-03-795. Washington, D.C.: July 15, 2003.

Natural Gas: Analysis of Changes in Market Price. GAO-03-46. Washington, D.C.: December 18, 2002.

SEC and CFTC: Most Fines Collected, but Improvements Needed in the Use of Treasury's Collection Service. GAO-01-900. Washington, D.C.: July 16, 2001.

Energy Markets: Results of Studies Assessing High Electricity Prices in California. GAO-01-857. Washington, D.C.: June 29, 2001.

Commodity Exchange Act: Issues Related to the Regulation of Electronic Trading Systems. GAO/GGD-00-99. Washington, D.C.: May 5, 2000.

CFTC and SEC: Issues Related to the Shad-Johnson Jurisdictional Accord. GAO/GGD-00-89. Washington, D.C.: April 6, 2000.

Financial Regulatory Coordination: The Role and Functioning of the President's Working Group. GAO/GGD-00-46. Washington, D.C.: January 21, 2000.

The Commodity Exchange Act: Issues Related to the Commodity Futures Trading Commission's Reauthorization. GAO/GGD-99-74. Washington, D.C.: May 5, 1999.

CFTC Enforcement: Actions Taken to Strengthen the Division of Enforcement. GAO/GGD-98-193. Washington, D.C.: August 28, 1998.

OTC Derivatives: Additional Oversight Could Reduce Costly Sales Practice Disputes. GAO/GGD-98-5. Washington, D.C.: October 2, 1997.

CFTC/SEC Enforcement Programs: Status and Potential Impact of a Merger. GAO/T-GGD-96-36. Washington, D.C.: October 25, 1995.

Financial Market Regulation: Benefits and Risks of Merging SEC and CFTC. GAO/T-GGD-95-153. Washington, D.C.: May 3, 1995.

Energy Security and Policy: Analysis of the Pricing of Crude Oil and Petroleum Products. GAO/RCED-93-17. Washington, D.C.: March 19, 1993.

Securities and Futures: How the Markets Developed and How They Are Regulated. GAO/GGD-86-26. Washington, D.C.: May 15, 1986.

End Notes

[1] Our analysis of energy prices and energy financial markets generally is limited to the period from January 2002 through December 2006. A "derivative" is a financial instrument, traded on- or off-exchange, the price of which for energy directly depends on the value of one or more underlying energy commodities. Derivatives involve the trading of rights or obligations on the basis of the underlying product, but they do not directly transfer property.

[2] CFTC's technical definition of a "futures contract" encompasses the following characteristics: (1) the contract price is determined at initiation of the contract; (2) the contract obligates each party to the contract to fulfill the contract at the specified price; (3) the contract is used to assume or shift price risk; and (4) the delivery obligation may be satisfied by delivery or offset (i.e., liquidating a purchase of futures contracts through the sale of an equal number of contracts of the same delivery month, or liquidating a short sale of futures through the purchase of an equal number of contracts of the same delivery month). A futures contract is a type of derivative.

[3] CFTC defines "hedge fund" as a private investment fund or pool that trades and invests in various assets, such as securities, commodities, currency, and derivatives, on behalf of its clients, typically wealthy individuals. In a "commodity index fund," prices are tied to the price of a basket of various commodity futures.

[4] See section 3 of the Commodity Exchange Act, 7 U.S.C. § 5 (2004).

[5] The LTRS includes the daily reports filed with CFTC showing the futures and options positions of traders that hold positions at or above specific exchange or CFTC-set reporting levels. Commodity traders or brokers that carry these accounts must make daily reports about the size of the position by commodity, by delivery month, and by whether the position is controlled by a commercial or noncommercial trader. Commercial participants generally are those that are engaged in business activities—including producing, merchandising, or processing a cash commodity or managing risk—that hedge using the futures or options markets. Noncommercial participants do not have an interest in the underlying commodity but trade in the energy futures markets to realize a profit.

[6] The CEA defines "exempt commodity" as a commodity that is "not an excluded commodity or an agricultural commodity." 7 U.S.C. § 1a(14). In practice, this definition primarily encompasses energy and metal commodities.

[7] In October 2005, NYMEX began to offer a new futures contract for reformulated gasoline blendstock known as "RB." This new contract traded alongside the existing gasoline contract known as "HU" until January 2007, when NYMEX discontinued trading in that contract.

[8] CFTC economists used the term "managed money traders" to describe a large category of speculative traders. See Michael S. Haigh, Jana Hranaiova, and James A. Overdahl, "Price Dynamics, Price Discovery and Large Futures Trader Interactions in the Energy Complex," U.S. Commodity Futures Trading Commission, Office of the Chief Economist, April 28, 2005, draft working paper available on CFTC's Web site. As stated in the paper, the views expressed therein are those of the authors and do not reflect the views of CFTC or its staff.

[9] CPOs are individuals or firms in businesses similar to investment trusts or syndicates that solicit or accept funds, securities, or property for the purpose of trading futures or commodity options. CTAs are individuals or firms that, for pay, issue analyses or reports concerning commodities, including the advisability of trading futures or commodity options. For the

purposes of the working paper, the authors used the term "managed money traders" to include all registered CPOs and CTAs.

[10] To account for the effects of inflation on prices, prices are adjusted to reflect prices in the base year of 2006.

[11] This scenario assumes that minimal costs are associated with holding the oil over the 2-week period.

[12] Futures Trading Practices Act of 1992 (Pub. L. No. 102-546 (Oct. 28, 1992)). Among other things, this act added a new provision to the CEA authorizing the commission, by rule, regulation, or order, to exempt any agreement, contract, or transaction, or class thereof, when entered into between "appropriate persons" from the exchange-trading, or any other, requirement of the act (other than the provision establishing CFTC's jurisdiction). Pub. L. No. 102-546 § 502. In April 1993, CFTC promulgated a final order generally exempting from the CEA qualifying energy contracts entered by commercial participants and certain other specified entities. 58 Fed. Reg. 21286 (Apr. 20, 1993).

[13] Pub. L. No. 106-554 § 1(a)(5), title 1 §§ 103-106 (Dec. 21, 2000).

[14] Another type of futures exchange that is subject to CFTC regulatory oversight is a derivatives transaction execution facility, which is a trading facility that limits access to mostly institutional traders rather than retail traders. Like a futures market, a derivatives transaction execution facility must register with CFTC but is subject to less regulation. To date, no exchange has applied to register as such a facility.

[15] President's Working Group on Financial Markets, *Over-the-Counter Derivatives Markets and the Commodity Exchange Act* (Nov. 9, 1999). Members of the President's Working Group on Financial Markets include the Chairman of CFTC, the Secretary of the Treasury, the Chairman of the Board of Governors of the Federal Reserve, and the Chairman of SEC.

[16] GAO, *Financial Regulation: Industry Changes Prompt Need to Reconsider U.S. Regulatory Structure*, GAO-05-61 (Washington, D.C.: Oct. 6, 2004).

[17] CFTC's other major operating units are the Office of the Chief Economist, Office of the General Counsel, and Office of the Executive Director. A derivatives clearing organization is a clearinghouse or similar organization that enables each party to a transaction to substitute the credit of the clearinghouse for the credit of the parties, provides for the settlement or netting of obligations from the transaction, or otherwise provides services mutualizing or transferring the credit risk from the transaction.

[18] Futures commission merchants are individuals, associations, partnerships, corporations, and trusts that solicit or accept orders for the purchase or sale of any commodity for future delivery on or subject to the rules of any exchange and that accept payment from or extend credit to those whose orders are accepted.

[19] As of January 1, 2007, CFTC closed its Minneapolis field office.

[20] Because energy commodities are related, specific types of events or conditions may affect all four energy commodities in a similar fashion. For example, the supply and demand fundamentals for crude oil have a direct effect on the supply, demand, and price of gasoline and heating oil because they are refined from crude oil. Crude oil market fundamentals also may affect natural gas because some consumers can use it as a substitute for crude oil products. If the price of crude oil rises, demand for natural gas as a substitute may rise, thereby increasing its price. However, natural gas prices are not always closely related to crude oil prices.

[21] The OPEC members are Algeria, Angola, Indonesia, Iran, Iraq, Kuwait, Libya, Nigeria, Qatar, Saudi Arabia, the United Arab Emirates, and Venezuela. Http://www.eia.doe.gov/emeu/cabs/AOMC/Overview.html.

[22] GAO, *Motor Fuels: Understanding the Factors That Influence the Retail Price of Gasoline*, GAO-05-525SP (Washington, D.C.: May 2005).

[23] GAO, *Energy Markets: Factors Contributing to Higher Gasoline Prices*, GAO-06-412T (Washington, D.C.: Feb. 1, 2006); and GAO-05-525SP.

[24] GAO-06-412T.

[25] GAO, *Gasoline Markets: Special Gasoline Blends Reduce Emissions and Improve Air Quality, but Complicate Supply and Contribute to Higher Prices*, GAO-05-421 (Washington, D.C.: June 17, 2005).

[26] GAO-05-525SP.

[27] Mark N. Cooper, *The Role of Supply, Demand and Financial Commodity Markets in the Natural Gas Price Spiral*, prepared for Midwest Attorneys General Natural Gas Working Group (Illinois, Iowa, Missouri, and Wisconsin: March 2006).

[28] The CFTC report did not look at the effects of recent trends in volume or the number of large traders on prices.

[29] "Standard deviation" is a measure of the dispersion of a set of data around its mean. When used to measure volatility, standard deviation measures the dispersion of daily percentage price changes around the average percentage price change.

[30] CFTC collects data on traders holding positions at or above specific reporting levels set by the commission. This information is collected as part of CFTC's LTRS.

[31] Senate's Permanent Subcommittee on Investigations, Committee on Homeland Security and Governmental Affairs, *The Role of Market Speculation in Rising Oil and Gas Prices: A Need to Put the Cop Back on the Beat*, S. Prt. 109-65, 109th Cong., 2nd Sess. (June 27, 2006).

[32] The Bank for International Settlements is an international organization that fosters international monetary and financial cooperation and serves as a bank for central banks.

[33] The "notional amount" is the amount upon which payments between parties to certain types of derivatives contracts are based. The notional amount is not exchanged between the parties, but instead represents a hypothetical underlying quantity upon which payment obligations are computed. The Bank for International Settlements data on OTC derivatives include forwards, swaps, and options.

[34] The CEA antimanipulation and antifraud prohibitions do not apply to excluded derivative and swap transactions. 7 U.S.C. § 2(d)–(g). The antimanipulation prohibitions apply to off-exchange transactions in exempt commodities. The antifraud provisions apply to transactions in exempt commodities only under particular circumstances.

[35] 17 C.F.R. § 36.3; see 7 U.S.C. § 2(h)(4)(D).

[36] On June 22, 2007, CFTC published for comment a proposed rule that, among other things, is intended to clarify that a person holding or controlling reportable positions on a futures exchange must keep records of and make available to CFTC information about all of the trader's transactions in the commodity reported, including any transactions in the exempt commercial markets, such as OTC energy derivatives. 72 Fed. Reg. 34413 (June 22, 2007).

[37] 7 U.S.C. § 7. Part 38 of the CFTC rules sets forth the procedures and criteria for designation as a contract market. Among other things, these procedures and criteria include guidance on compliance with CEA designation criteria and acceptable practices in compliance with the core principles. See 17 C.F.R. Part 38.

[38] 7 U.S.C. § 7a-2(c)(3).

[39] 17 C.F.R. Parts 155, 166.

[40] Under a special call for 2(h)(3) (exempt commodity) markets, ICE, which is not subject to the oversight CFTC has over futures markets such as NYMEX, is providing large trader data to CFTC. The COT report was first published monthly in 1962. Since 1995, it has been available for free at CFTC's Web site; since 2000, it has been published weekly.

[41] 71 Fed. Reg. 35627, 35630-31 (June 21, 2006).

[42] 17 C.F.R. § 36.3. CFTC's antifraud authority under the CEA applies only to transactions within the commission's authority. Therefore, CFTC's antifraud authority would not apply to cash or forward transactions on exempt commercial markets.

[43] As discussed in footnote 54, a ruling by one federal appellate court means that the CEA antifraud provision may not apply to off-exchange transactions conducted on a principal-to-principal basis.

[44] These requirements are contained in CFTC rule 36.3.

[45] 7 U.S.C. § 2(h)(4)(D).

[46] 7 U.S.C. § 2(h)(5).

[47] In a recent CFTC complaint filed against Amaranth Advisors, LLC; Amaranth Advisors (Calgary), ULC; and Brian Hunter, CFTC alleges that the defendants attempted to manipulate the price of natural gas contracts on NYMEX in 2006. *CFTC v. Amaranth Advisors, LLC*, '07 CIV 6682 (SD NY, July 25, 2007).

[48] ICE also trades financially settled contracts.

[49] 7 U.S.C. § 2(h)(3). The term "eligible commercial entity" is defined at 7 U.S.C. § 1a(11). In general, these participants are entities such as financial institutions, commodity pools, or large businesses that, by virtue of their regulatory or financial status, are permitted to engage in transactions not available to other participants, such as retail customers.

[50] 7 U.S.C. § 2(h)(2),(4). As we have previously noted in this report, if the electronic trading facility upon which these exempt contracts are traded becomes a significant price discovery market, it may be subject to CFTC rules on the timely dissemination of pricing data and trading volume and information. Also, a facility relying on the exemption must notify the commission of its intent to operate; provide the name of the facility; describe the types of commodity categories being traded; identify its clearing facility, if any; certify that the facility will comply with the terms of the exemptions; certify that the owners of the trading facility are not otherwise statutorily disqualified under the CEA; either provide the commission with real-time access to its trading system and protocols, or provide CFTC with such reports as it may request; maintain books and records for 5 years; agree to provide the commission with specific information on a special call basis; agree to submit to CFTC's subpoena authority; agree to comply with all applicable laws and require the same of its participants; and not represent that the facility is registered with or in any way recognized by CFTC. 17 C.F.R. § 36.3; see 7 U.S.C. § 2(h)(5).

[51] Eva Gutierrez, *A Framework for the Surveillance of Derivatives Activities*, International Monetary Fund Working Paper WP/05/61 (Washington, D.C.: March 2005).

[52] *Over-the-Counter Derivatives Markets and the Commodity Exchange Act.*

[53] As stated by CFTC, the purpose of the proposed regulation is to make it explicit that persons holding or controlling reportable positions on a reporting market must retain books and records and make available to the commission upon request any pertinent information with respect to all other positions and transactions in the commodity in which the trader has a reportable position, including positions held or controlled or transactions executed over-the-counter or pursuant to sections 2(d), 2(g) or 2(h)(1)–(2) of the CEA or part 35 of the commission's regulations, on exempt commercial markets operating pursuant to sections 2(h)(3)–(5) of the CEA, on exempt boards of trade operating pursuant to Section 5d of the CEA, and on foreign boards of trade (hereinafter referred to collectively as non-reporting transactions); and to make the regulation clearer and more complete with respect to hedging activity. The purpose of the amendments is to clarify CFTC's regulatory reporting requirements for such traders. 72 Fed. Reg. 34413.

[54] Section 4b of the CEA is CFTC's main antifraud authority. In a November 2000 decision, the 7th Circuit Court of Appeals ruled that CFTC only could use section 4b in intermediated transactions—those involving a broker. *Commodity Trend Service, Inc. v. CFTC*, 233 F.3d 981, 991-992 (7th Cir. 2000). As amended by the CFMA, the CEA permits off-exchange futures and options transactions that are done on a principal-to-principal basis, such as energy transactions pursuant to CEA sections 2(h)(1) and 2(h)(3). According to CFTC, House and Senate CFTC reauthorization bills introduced during the 109th Congress (H.R. 4473 and S. 1566) would have amended section 4b to clarify that Congress intends for CFTC to enforce section 4b in connection with off-exchange principal-to-principal futures transactions, including exempt commodity transactions in energy under section 2(h) as well as all transactions conducted on derivatives transaction execution facilities.

[55] Commodity Futures Trading Commission, *Performance and Accountability Report: Fiscal Year 2005* (Washington, D.C.: November 2005).

[56] The LTRS data also can be used to identify violations of speculative position limits. The CEA authorizes CFTC to impose limits on the size of speculative positions in futures markets to protect futures markets from excessive speculation that can cause unreasonable or unwarranted price fluctuations. Exchanges establish speculative limits for energy products. Violations of exchange speculative limits may be charged by the commission as violations of section 4a of the CEA, if the exchange rules have been approved by the commission.

[57] *In re Indiana Farm Bureau Cooperative Association,* [1982-1984 Transfer Binder] *Comm. Fut. L. Rep. (CCH) P21,796 at 27,281,* n.2 (CFTC: Dec. 17, 1982) (explaining that "[i]n order to prove a successful manipulation, it is necessary to demonstrate that the accused intentionally caused an 'artificial price,' that is, a price which does not reflect the market or economic forces of supply and demand.") One of the purposes of the CEA is to prevent market manipulation. *Curran v. Merrill Lynch, Pierce, Fenner & Smith, Inc.,* 622 F.2d 216, 235 (6th Cir. 1980) (noting the "Congressional intent [in enacting the act] to protect the public from fraud and price manipulation"). Sections 6(c), 6(d), and 9(a)(2) of the CEA, 7 U.S.C. §§ 9, 13b, 13(a)(2), make it illegal for any person to manipulate or attempt to manipulate the market price of any commodity, in interstate commerce, or for future delivery on or subject to the rules of any registered entity (including any contract market), or to corner or attempt to corner any such commodity or knowingly deliver or cause to be delivered false, misleading, or knowingly inaccurate reports concerning crop or market information or conditions that affect or tend to affect the price of any commodity in interstate commerce. As a result of the commission carrying out the statutory mandate through enforcement actions and administrative decisions, a body of federal and commission case law has emerged to define manipulation under the act. Generally, the following factors are assessed in manipulation cases: (1) that the accused had the ability to influence market prices, (2) that the accused specifically intended to do so, (3) that artificial prices existed, and (4) that the accused caused an artificial price. *In re Cox,* [1986-1987 Transfer Binder] Comm. Fut. L. Rep. (CCH) ¶ 23,786 at 34,061 (CFTC: July 15, 1987).

[58] A position is a long or short interest in the market in the form of one or more contracts.

[59] GAO, *Long-Term Capital Management: Regulators Need to Focus Greater Attention on Systemic Risk,* GAO/GGD-00-3 (Washington, D.C.: Oct. 29, 1999).

[60] Section 9(a)(2) of the CEA prohibits "(a)ny person to manipulate or attempt to manipulate the price of any commodity in interstate commerce, or for future delivery on or subject to the rules of any registered entity, or to corner or attempt to corner any such commodity or knowingly to deliver or cause to be delivered for transmission through the mails or interstate commerce by telegraph, telephone, wireless, or other means of communication false or misleading or knowingly inaccurate reports concerning crop or market information or conditions that affect or tend to affect the price of any commodity interstate commerce...."

[61] Section 9 of the CEA, 7 U.S.C. § 13(a)(2), makes it a felony for any person to manipulate or attempt to manipulate the price of any commodity in interstate commerce as well as the prices of futures contracts.

[62] See Order to Show Cause and Notice of Proposed Penalties, FERC Docket No. IN07-26-000 (July 26, 2007).

[63] *CFTC v. BP Products North America, Inc.,* No. 06C 3503 (N.D. Ill. filed June 28, 2006).

[64] GAO reports cited in the PART assessment: CFTC Enforcement: *Actions Taken to Strengthen the Division of Enforcement,* GAO/GGD-98-193 (Washington, D.C.: Aug. 23, 1998); *SEC and CFTC Fines Follow-Up Collection Programs Are Improving, but Further Steps Are Warranted,* GAO-03-795 (Washington, D.C.: July 15, 2003); *Results Act: Observations on CFTC's Annual Performance Plan,* GAO/T-GGD-99-10 (Washington, D.C.: Oct. 8, 1998); and *Results Act: Observations on CFTC's Strategic Plan,* GAO/T-GGD-98-17 (Washington, D.C.: Oct. 22, 1997).

[65] GAO, *Results Oriented Government: GPRA Has Established a Solid Foundation for Achieving Greater Results,* GAO-04-594T (Washington, D.C.: Mar. 31, 2004).

[66] GAO, *Program Evaluation: OMB's PART Reviews Increased Agencies' Attention to Improving Evidence of Program Results*, GAO-07-67 (Washington, D.C.: Oct. 28, 2005).

[67] The street book is a daily record showing details of each futures and option transaction, including date, price quantity, market, commodity, future, and name of the person for whom the trade was made.

[68] There is a NYMEX BCC and COMEX BCC. A BCC meeting is scheduled to meet every month, alternatively for NYMEX and COMEX.

[69] NYMEX said that not all inquiries become formal investigations. For example, in 2005, the Market Surveillance area reported 887 cases, but the vase majority of these were routine position limit reviews, inquires about exchange for physical and exchange of futures for swaps, and unreported reviews that never became formal investigations. The Trade Practice area logs inquiries that may or may not evolve to formal investigations.

In: Energy Prices: Supply, Demand …   ISBN: 978-1-60741-374-5
Editor: John T. Perry   © 2010 Nova Science Publishers, Inc.

Chapter 3

REGULATION OF ENERGY DERIVATIVES

Mark Jickling

SUMMARY

After the collapse of Enron Corp. in late 2001, that company's activities came under intense scrutiny. Much of its business consisted of trading financial contracts whose value was derived from changes in energy prices. Enron's derivatives trading was largely "over-the-counter" (OTC) and unregulated: little information about transactions was available. Trading in energy derivatives rebounded after a post-Enron slump, and much of the market remains unregulated. This "regulatory gap" strikes some observers as dangerous for two reasons. First, the absence of government oversight may facilitate abusive trading or price manipulation. A June 2007 report by the Senate Permanent Subcommittee on Investigations concluded that excessive speculation by the Amaranth hedge fund, which failed in 2006, had distorted natural gas prices. Second, the failure of a large derivatives dealer could conceivably trigger disruptions of supplies and prices in physical energy markets (though the effect was minor in the Enron case).

A number of bills before the 110th Congress would give the Commodity Futures Trading Commission (CFTC) enhanced authority to regulate certain energy trades on markets other than the regulated futures exchanges. H.R. 2419 (the Farm Bill), enacted as P.L. 110-234 on May 22, 2008, over the President's veto, will impose exchange-like regulations on electronic over-the-counter markets that play a significant role in setting energy prices. This report summarizes energy derivatives regulation and proposed legislation. It will be updated as developments warrant.

Energy derivatives — financial contracts whose value is linked to changes in the price of some energy product — are traded in several kinds of markets: the futures exchanges and the off-exchange, or over-the-counter market. The New York Mercantile Exchange (Nymex) is the leading U.S. market for futures contracts based on prices of crude oil, natural gas, heating oil, and gasoline. Futures exchanges — called "designated contract markets" — are regulated by the Commodity Futures Trading Commission (CFTC) under the Commodity Exchange Act (CEA). The CEA imposes a range of mandates on the exchanges (and on futures industry personnel) regarding record keeping (including an audit trail for all trades), registration requirements, market surveillance, financial standards, sales practices, handling of customer funds, and so on.

The second trading venue for energy derivatives is the off-exchange, or over-thecounter (OTC) market. Unlike the futures market, there is no centralized marketplace for OTC derivatives. Instead, a number of firms act as dealers, offering to enter into contracts with others who wish to manage their risk exposure to energy prices. OTC contracts based on energy products are generally exempt from regulation under the CEA, so long as the contracts are offered only to "eligible contract participants," defined as financial institutions, professional traders, institutional investors, governmental units, and businesses or individuals who exceed various asset and income thresholds. The law assumes that sophisticated parties such as these do not need the investor protections that government regulation provides for small public customers of the futures exchanges.

In recent years, a hybrid form of market has emerged, which resembles the exchanges in that multiple parties can trade on an electronic platform, but which has been largely exempt from CFTC regulation. These markets, known as "exempt commercial markets," must notify the CFTC before they begin operations, and provide certain basic information about themselves, but they are not required to monitor trading, publish data on trading volumes or prices, or enforce CEA prohibitions against fraud or manipulation. Before the passage of P.L. 110-234, the CFTC had limited jurisdiction, other than enforcement authority over manipulation and fraud.

To traders, whether they are speculating on price changes in search of profit or using derivatives to protect themselves from the price risk associated with producing or purchasing physical energy commodities, these markets are basically interchangeable.

HISTORICAL DEVELOPMENT OF DERIVATIVES REGULATION

In 1974, Congress observed that derivatives trading was about to expand from its traditional base in farm commodities into financial futures — contracts based on bonds, interest rates, currencies, and so on. To ensure that derivatives traders received the same protections whether they were trading pork bellies or T-bonds, P.L. 93-463 created the CFTC to oversee all derivatives trading, regardless of the nature of the underlying commodity. The CFTC was given exclusive jurisdiction: all contracts that were "in the character of" futures contracts had to be traded on a CFTC-regulated futures exchange.

There were two major exceptions to this exchange-trading requirement. Forward contracts, where actual delivery of the commodity would take place at the expiration of the contract, were considered cash sales and not subject to the CEA. Second, the socalled Treasury Amendment (part of the same law that created the CFTC) specified that contracts based on foreign currencies or U.S. Treasury securities could be traded offexchange. Existing markets in these instruments had long used futures-like contracts and appeared to function well without direct government regulation; Treasury saw no public interest in bringing them under the new CFTC.

During the 1980s, a market in OTC derivatives evolved, utilizing swap contracts that served exactly the same economic functions as futures. The first swaps were based on currencies and interest rates; later, OTC contracts based on commodity (including energy) prices were introduced. These OTC markets were well established before the CFTC made any move to assert its jurisdiction, despite the fact that swaps were clearly "in the character of" futures contracts. The potential CFTC jurisdiction, however, created legal uncertainty for the swaps industry: if a court had ruled that a swap was in fact an illegal, off-exchange futures contract, trillions of dollars in outstanding swaps could have been invalidated. This might have caused chaos in financial markets, as swaps users would suddenly be exposed to the risks they had used derivatives to avoid.

The CFTC issued a swaps exemption in 1989, holding that the CEA gave it authority to regulate swaps, but that it would not do so as long as they differed from futures contracts in certain enumerated respects. In 1992, Congress gave the CFTC additional authority to exempt OTC contracts (P.L. 102-546). In response, the CFTC modified the 1989 swaps exemption in 1993, and also issued a specific exemption for OTC derivatives based on energy products.[1] Under the 1993 exemption, OTC energy derivatives would not be regulated if all trading was between principals whose business involved the physical energy commodities underlying the derivatives, if all contracts were negotiated as to their material terms (unlike futures contracts, where terms are standardized), and if all contracts were held to maturity (rather than traded rapidly, as futures are).

This exemption was a matter of regulation, not statute. In May 1998, the CFTC issued a "concept release" that indicated that it was considering the possibility of extending features of exchange regulation to the OTC market. The release solicited comments on whether regulation of OTC derivatives should be modified in light of developments in the marketplace. Among the questions were whether the existing prohibitions on fraud and manipulation were sufficient to protect the public, and whether the CFTC should consider additional terms and conditions relating to registration, capital, internal controls, sales practices, record keeping, or reporting.

The concept release drew strong opposition from the swaps industry and from other regulators, especially the Federal Reserve. In December 1998, Congress included in the Omnibus Appropriations Act (P.L. 105-277) a provision directing the CFTC not to propose or issue any new regulations affecting swap contracts before March 31, 1999. In November 1999, the President's Working Group on Financial Markets issued a report entitled "Over-the-Counter Derivatives Markets and the Commodity Exchange Act." The report recommended that, to remove uncertainty about the legal and regulatory status of the OTC market, bilateral transactions between sophisticated parties that do not involve physical commodities with finite supplies should be excluded from the Commodity Exchange Act; that is, the CFTC should have no jurisdiction. While the Working Group's report made a distinction between financial commodities and those with finite supplies, and suggested that continuing CEA jurisdiction was appropriate for the latter, the report did *not* recommend that the CFTC should rescind its exemption of OTC energy derivatives. In other words, the Working Group saw no immediate problem with the unregulated status of OTC markets in energy derivatives.

In 2000, Congress passed the Commodity Futures Modernization Act of 2000 (P.L. 106-554, H.R. 5660). That legislation established three classes of commodities. First, financial variables (interest rates, stock indexes, currencies, etc.) are defined as "excluded commodities," and OTC contracts based on these are not subject to the CEA (provided that trading is restricted to "eligible contract participants," that is, not marketed to small investors).

Second, there is no statutory exemption for derivative contracts based on agricultural commodities: these remain under CFTC jurisdiction. Finally, there is an "all other" category — "exempt commodities" — which includes energy products. Contracts in exempt commodities can be traded in the OTC market without CFTC regulation provided that no small investors participate. However, certain antifraud and antimanipulation provisions of the CEA continue to apply. If an OTC exchange is created — defined in the law as an "electronic trading facility" where multiple buyers and sellers may post bids and trade with each other — the CFTC has some oversight jurisdiction and may require disclosure of certain market information.

In summary, the OTC energy derivatives market developed outside CFTC jurisdiction in the late 1980s and early 1990s, despite the CEA's apparent prohibition of such a market. As with financial OTC derivatives, however, the CFTC never challenged the legality of this off-exchange market. As concerns about legal uncertainty mounted, the CFTC in 1993 issued an exemption stating that certain OTC energy transactions did not fall under the CEA. In 2000, Congress essentially codified this exemption, by including energy in the category of "exempt commodities." This removed them from even the possibility of CFTC regulation, except for a limited antifraud and manipulation jurisdiction and some oversight if the market for OTC contracts should evolve into an exchange-like market. Thus, the 2000 legislation did not deregulate the OTC energy derivatives market; that market had been unregulated since its beginnings.

MANIPULATION IN ENERGY MARKETS

Since the value of derivatives contracts is linked to the price of the underlying commodity, traders who can manipulate commodity prices can reap huge profits. Manipulative strategies may involve either physical (spot) or derivatives markets, or both. Since the Enron scandal, regulators have taken numerous actions against several types of manipulation in energy markets.

In 2003, the CFTC charged Enron with manipulation of natural gas prices. The strategy was simple: Enron purchased an unusual number of contracts for spot gas, driving up prices by simultaneously increasing demand in the marketplace and making other traders think that there was some fundamental factor that favored higher prices. Enron settled CFTC charges by agreeing to pay a $35 million fine in 2004.

Ten energy companies have paid a total of $180 million in fines to settle CFTC charges that they manipulated natural gas prices in 2001 and 2002 by providing false data about supply levels to Platts, a private source of information on energy market conditions. The affected Platts reports sent false signals to other market participants that supplies were significantly tighter than expected, and prices rose (sharply, but briefly) as a result.

Enron and a number of other firms admitted to "gaming" the marketing system for electrical power in California in 2000, exacerbating price increases and shortages. The strategies included deceptive reporting of energy supplies on hand (to create the impression of shortages to drive up prices), disguising the source of electricity (to take advantage of variable pricing for in-state and out-of-state power), and in some cases actually closing power plants during times of tight supplies to drive up prices. Numerous firms and traders faced civil and criminal charges as a result of these manipulations.

In August 2006, the Amaranth hedge fund lost $2 billion in natural gas derivatives, and liquidated its entire $8 billion portfolio. A June 2007 staff report by the Senate Permanent Subcommittee on Investigations ("Excessive Speculation in the Natural Gas Market") found that the fund's collapse triggered a steep, unexpected decline in prices, and that Amaranth's large positions had caused significant price movements in the months before it failed. The report concludes that Amaranth was able to evade limits on the size of speculative positions (a key feature of the futures exchanges' anti-manipulation program) by shifting its trading from Nymex to exempt and unregulated markets.

As energy (and agricultural) commodity prices reached record highs in 2008, there was concern that financial speculators were driving prices up to levels not justified by fundamentals of supply and demand. It is common to speak of a "speculative premium," or a "bubble," in the price of oil, but there is no sure methodology for determining what a commodity price "ought to be" based on the fundamentals. Some analysts believe the price of oil is headed higher; others think a sharp fall is possible.

LEGISLATIVE PROPOSALS ON DERIVATIVES REGULATION

Since Enron, the regulatory status of OTC energy derivatives has been much debated. In the 110th Congress, H.R. 594 would enhance the CFTC's authority over the OTC energy market and require reporting of trade data necessary to prevent price manipulation. H.R. 3009 would impose reporting requirements on certain natural gas traders. H.R. 4066, S. 577, S. 2058, and S. 2991 would require the reporting of large positions in energy commodities by traders in the OTC market and on foreign futures exchanges that are accessible via terminals located in the United States. S. 2058 and H.R. 4066 authorize the CFTC to establish core principles for exempt commercial markets like ICE, which would require them to monitor and enforce rules against manipulation and excessive speculation.

On May 22, 2008, Congress enacted the farm bill (H.R. 2419; P.L. 110-234) over the President's veto. Title XIII included provisions reauthorizing the CFTC and creates a new regulatory regime for certain OTC energy derivatives markets, subjecting them to a number of exchange-like regulations. The provisions apply to "electronic trading facilities" — markets where multiple buyers and sellers are able to post orders and execute transactions over an electronic network. If the CFTC determines that these markets, currently exempt from most regulation, play a significant role in setting energy prices, they will be required to register with the CFTC and comply with several regulatory core principles aimed at curbing manipulation and excessive speculation (including the establishment and enforcement of position limits). They will be required to publish and/or report to the CFTC information relating to prices, trading volume, and size of positions held by speculators and hedgers.

These new regulatory requirements apply only to electronic markets that have come to resemble the regulated futures exchanges. Bilateral OTC derivative contracts between two principals (e.g., between a swap dealer and an institutional investor), that are not executed on a trading facility where multiple bids and offers are displayed, will continue to be largely exempt from CFTC regulation.

S. 2991 would raise the margin requirements for crude oil futures contracts. Margin is the amount of money that a trader must post with the exchange to buy or sell a single futures contract: for crude oil, the Nymex margin is currently $10,463 per contract (each contract represents 1,000 barrels of oil). (Margin requirements are normally set by the futures exchanges.) Higher margins raise the cost of trading: the theory is that higher costs will drive out speculation, moderating price volatility, and perhaps easing upward pressure on prices themselves. Empirical research, however, has not established a strong link between margin levels (or speculation in general) and price volatility.

Current concerns about excessive speculation in energy raise basic issues about derivatives markets. The CFTC does not believe that energy markets are being manipulated, but that they are responding to traders' expectations of future prices, which is their proper function. The CFTC's conception of manipulation, requires that a single trader (or group of traders) amass a market position that enables them to willfully distort or dictate prices in defiance of the fundamentals. The CFTC's observation that it cannot detect any elements of such a classic "corner" or "squeeze" behind today's high prices, and that therefore the markets are functioning well, does little to reassure the many observers who believe that a flood of money from hedge funds, Wall Street firms, pension funds, endowments, and other institutional investors has driven prices artificially high. To these observers, excessive financial speculation is in itself a form of manipulation, even though it does not meet the legal definition.

A fundamental issue is whether speculation causes prices to become more volatile. Empirical research suggests that *in general* it does not, but financial markets in recent years have witnessed several episodes of price bubbles — dot.com stocks, residential real estate, mortgage-backed bonds — indicating that markets at times generate prices that are not supported by fundamental factors of supply and demand. Attempts to limit the influence of speculators include S. 2991's call for higher margin requirements in energy futures. More stringent measures are available: India recently banned trading of agricultural futures contracts. It is not certain, however, that a market where speculation is restrained will be less volatile than the ones we have now, nor that we have a better model for setting prices than a market where traders of all kinds pool their information by taking risky financial positions based on their expectations of future price trends.

End Notes

[1] "Exemption for Certain Products Involving Energy Products," Federal Register, vol. 58, April 20, 1993, p. 21286.

In: Energy Prices: Supply, Demand …   ISBN: 978-1-60741-374-5
Editor: John T. Perry   © 2010 Nova Science Publishers, Inc.

Chapter 4

COMMODITY FUTURES TRADING COMMISSION TRENDS IN ENERGY DERIVATIVES MARKETS RAISE QUESTIONS ABOUT CFTC'S OVERSIGHT

Orice M. Williams

Why GAO Did This Study

Energy prices for crude oil, heating oil, unleaded gasoline, and natural gas have risen substantially since 2002, generating questions about the role derivatives markets have played and the scope of the Commodity Futures Trading Commission's (CFTC) authority. This testimony focuses on (1) trends and patterns in the futures and physical energy markets and their effects on energy prices, (2) the scope of CFTC's regulatory authority, and (3) the effectiveness of CFTC's monitoring and detection of abuses in energy markets. The testimony is based on the GAO report, *Commodity Futures Trading Commission: Trends in Energy Derivatives Markets Raise Questions about CFTC's Oversight* (GAO-08-25, October 19, 2007). For this work, GAO analyzed futures and large trader data and interviewed market participants, experts, and officials at six federal agencies.

What GAO Recommends

As part of CFTC's reauthorization process, GAO recommended that Congress consider exploring the scope of the agency's authority over energy derivatives trading, in particular for trading in exempt commercial markets. In addition, GAO recommends that CFTC improve the usefulness of the information provided to the public, better document its monitoring activities, and develop more outcome-oriented performance measures for its enforcement program. CFTC generally agreed with GAO's recommendations.

To view the full product, including the scope and methodology, click on GAO-08-174T. For more information, contact Orice Williams at (202) 512-8678 or williamso@gao.gov. Highlights of GAO-08-174T, a testimony before the Subcommittee on General Farm Commodities and Risk Management, Committee on Agriculture, House of Representatives

What GAO Found

Various trends in both the physical and futures markets have affected energy prices. Specifically, tight supply and rising demand in the physical markets contributed to higher prices as global demand for oil has risen rapidly while spare production capacity has fallen since 2002. Moreover, increased political instability in some of the major oil-producing countries has threatened the supply of oil. During this period, increasing numbers of noncommercial participants became active in the futures markets (including hedge funds) and the volume of energy futures contracts traded also increased. Simultaneously, the volume of energy derivatives traded outside of traditional futures exchanges increased significantly. Because these developments took place concurrently, the effect of any individual trend or factor on energy prices is unclear.

Under the authority granted by the Commodity Exchange Act (CEA), CFTC focuses its oversight primarily on the operations of traditional futures exchanges, such as the New York Mercantile Exchange, Inc. (NYMEX), where energy futures are traded. Increasing amounts of energy derivatives trading also occur on markets that are largely exempt from CFTC oversight. For example, exempt commercial markets conduct trading on electronic facilities between large, sophisticated participants. In addition, considerable trading occurs in over-the-counter (OTC) markets in which eligible parties enter into contracts directly, without using an exchange. While CFTC can act to enforce the CEA's antimanipulation and antifraud provisions for activities that occur in exempt commercial and OTC markets, some market observers question whether CFTC needs broader authority to more routinely oversee these markets. CFTC is currently examining the effects of trading in the regulated and exempt energy markets on price discovery and the scope of its authority over these markets—an issue that will warrant further examination as part of the CFTC reauthorization process.

CFTC conducts daily surveillance of trading on NYMEX that is designed to detect and deter fraudulent or abusive trading practices involving energy futures contracts. To detect abusive practices, such as potential manipulation, CFTC uses various information sources and relies heavily on trading activity data for large market participants. Using this information, CFTC staff may pursue alleged abuse or manipulation. However, because the agency does not maintain complete records of all such allegations, determining the usefulness and extent of these activities is difficult. In addition, CFTC's performance measures for its enforcement program do not fully reflect the program's goals and purposes, which could be addressed by developing additional outcome-based performance measures that more fully reflect progress in meeting the program's overall goals. Because of changes and innovations in the market, the reports that CFTC receives on market activities may no longer be accurate because they use categories that do not adequately separate trading being done for different reasons by various market participants.

Mr. Chairman and Members of the Subcommittee:

I am pleased to be here today to discuss our recent report on the trading of derivatives for energy commodities, including crude oil and natural gas, and the Commodity Futures Trading Commission's (CFTC) oversight of these markets.[1] The expansion of derivatives trading in energy markets, particularly by participants such as hedge funds, and rapid growth in trading off regulated exchanges have raised questions about the quality and quantity of reporting on and oversight of these trading activities.[2]

Specifically, I will discuss (1) trends in the physical and energy derivatives markets and their effect on energy prices, (2) the scope of CFTC's authority for protecting market users in the trading of energy derivatives, and (3) CFTC's monitoring and detection of market abuses in energy futures markets. I should point out that our review was intended to identify trends in both the physical and derivatives energy markets and to provide information on the current regulatory structure for energy derivatives trading, including analyzing the various perspectives of market participants on these issues. While our report frames issues that need to be addressed, we do not offer specific policy solutions.

During the course of our review, we obtained and analyzed energy futures prices and trading volumes from the New York Mercantile Exchange, Inc. (NYMEX). Specifically, we collected data for crude oil, heating oil, natural gas, and unleaded gas from January 2002 through December 2006. We also analyzed data obtained from CFTC on market participants and the outstanding trading positions of different categories of traders. We reviewed publicly available information, including academic studies and reports and market data. Finally, we interviewed a broad range of market participants and observers, representatives of energy trading markets, and government regulators and agencies involved with the energy markets. This work was done in accordance with generally accepted government auditing standards.

SUMMARY

Physical and derivatives markets for crude oil, unleaded gasoline, heating oil, and natural gas have experienced substantial changes in recent years. Within the physical market, tight supply and rising global demand, ongoing political instability in oil-producing regions, limited refining capacity, and other supply disruptions all contributed to higher prices. While these changes were occurring in the physical markets, in the derivatives markets volatility of energy prices generally remained above historic averages for most of the period but declined during 2006 to levels at or near the historical average. Moreover, trading volumes for futures increased, at least in part because a growing number of managed-money traders (including hedge funds) began to see energy futures as attractive investment alternatives. Another change occurring during this time was the increased trading of energy derivatives outside the organized exchanges. Trading in these markets—specifically electronic commercial markets and over-the-counter (OTC) markets—is much less transparent than trading on futures exchanges, and comprehensive data are not available because these energy markets are not regulated. Given that the developments in the physical and derivatives markets were occurring simultaneously, determining their effect on energy prices is difficult. Continued monitoring of the various factors that affect market prices, and how those factors are changing, will be important in protecting the public and ensuring market integrity.

Energy derivatives are traded on futures exchanges and off-exchange in exempt commercial and OTC markets.[3] Exempt commercial markets are electronic trading facilities that trade exempt commodities, including energy commodities, on a principal-to-principal basis solely between commercial entities meeting certain eligibility requirements. In the OTC markets, parties meeting certain requirements can enter into bilateral energy derivatives transactions. Unlike the futures exchanges, which are subject to comprehensive oversight by CFTC, exempt commercial markets and OTC markets are not subject to general CFTC oversight, although CFTC can enforce the CEA's antimanipulation provisions and, where applicable, the antifraud provisions. To provide transparency about trading on the futures exchanges, CFTC routinely publicly reports aggregate information on trading by large commercial (such as oil companies, refineries, and other hedge traders) and noncommercial (such as hedge funds) participants that occurs on the exchanges. However, in the way the data are currently categorized, no distinction is made between commercial traders who use the exchanges to hedge their positions in the physical markets and those commercial traders, such as investment banks, who trade futures to hedge their trading in off-exchange derivatives. Given the developments and growth in the energy trading markets, questions have been raised over whether CFTC needs broader authority over the off-exchange derivative markets, particularly those involving exempt commodities and exempt commercial markets.

At an operational level, we also reported that while CFTC conducts reporting, surveillance, and enforcement activities in the energy markets to help provide transparency to the public, detect fraudulent or manipulative trading practices, and deter abuses, the effectiveness of these efforts is unclear. For example:

- Although CFTC monitors exchange trading activity through its surveillance program and gathers additional information from NYMEX officials, traders, or other sources to determine if further action is warranted, staff did not routinely document the results of these inquiries. Instead, they kept formal records of their findings only in cases in which improper trading was identified. As a result, CFTC may be limiting its opportunities to identify trends and its ability to measure the extent and usefulness of its monitoring activities.
- We also found that CFTC has successfully pursued energy-related cases, but we were not able to determine how effectively CFTC's

enforcement activities were in identifying violations and deterring misconduct because the agency lacked meaningful outcome-based measures.

Our report includes a matter for congressional consideration and three recommendations to CFTC. In light of recent developments and the uncertainty over the adequacy of CFTC's oversight, we recommend that Congress, as part of the CFTC reauthorization process, further explore whether the current regulatory structure for energy derivatives, in particular for those traded in exempt commercial markets, adequately provides for fair trading and accurate pricing of energy commodities. To improve the transparency of market activities and the functioning of CFTC's oversight, we recommend that CFTC reconsider how information it publishes in trading reports for energy products could be improved and CFTC has agreed to reexamine the classifications used in these reports. CFTC also agreed with our recommend-dations aimed at better documenting its surveillance activities and developing more outcome-based performance measures and has taken steps to implement them.

BACKGROUND

Energy commodities are bought and sold on both the physical and financial markets. The physical market includes the spot market where products such as crude oil or gasoline are bought and sold for immediate or near-term delivery by producers, wholesalers, and retailers. Spot transactions take place between commercial participants for a particular energy product for immediate delivery at a specific location. For example, the U.S. spot market for West Texas Intermediate crude oil is the pipeline hub near Cushing, Oklahoma, while a major spot market for natural gas operates at the Henry Hub near Erath, Louisiana. The prices set in the specific spot markets provide a reference point that buyers and sellers use to set the price for other types of the commodity traded at other locations.

In addition to the spot markets, derivatives based on energy commodities are traded in financial markets. The value of the derivative contract depends on the performance of the underlying asset—for example, crude oil or natural gas. Derivatives include futures, options, and swaps. Energy futures include standardized exchange-traded contracts for future delivery of a specific crude oil, heating oil, natural gas, or gasoline product at a particular spot market location. An exchange designated by CFTC as a contract market standardizes the contracts. The owner of an energy futures contract is obligated to buy or sell the commodity at a specified price and future date. However, the contractual obligation may be removed at any time before the contract expiration date if the owner sells or purchases other contracts with terms that offset the original contract. In practice, most futures contracts on NYMEX are liquidated via offset, so that physical delivery of the underlying commodity is relatively rare.

Market participants use futures markets to offset the risk caused by changes in prices, to discover commodity prices, and to speculate on price changes. Some buyers and sellers of energy commodities in the physical markets trade in futures contracts to offset or "hedge" the risks they face from price changes in the physical market. Exempt commercial markets and OTC derivatives are also used to hedge this risk. The ability to reduce their price risk is an important concern for buyers and sellers of energy commodities, because wide fluctuations in cash market prices introduce uncertainty for producers, distributors, and consumers of commodities and make investment planning, budgeting, and forecasting more difficult. To manage price risk, market participants may shift it to others more willing to assume the risk or to those having different risk situations. For example, if a petroleum refiner wants to lower its risk of losing money because of price volatility, it could lock in a price by selling futures contracts to deliver the gasoline in 6 months at a guaranteed price. Without futures contracts to manage risk, producers, refiners, and others would likely face greater uncertainty.

By establishing prices for future delivery, the futures market also helps buyers and sellers determine or "discover" the price of commodities in the physical markets, thus linking the two markets together. Markets are best able to perform price discovery when (1) participants have current information about the fundamental market forces of supply and demand, (2) large numbers of participants are active in the market, and (3) the market is transparent. Market participants monitor and analyze a myriad of information on the factors that currently affect and that they expect to affect the supply of and demand for energy commodities. With that information, participants buy or sell an energy commodity contract at the price they believe the commodity will sell for on the delivery date. The futures market, in effect, distills the diverse views of market participants into a single price. In turn, buyers and sellers of physical commodities may consider those predictions about future prices, among other factors, when setting prices on the spot and retail markets.

Other participants, such as investment banks and hedge funds, which do not have a commercial interest in the underlying commodities, generally use the futures market for profit. These speculators provide liquidity to the market but also take on risks that other participants, such as hedgers, seek to avoid. In addition, arbitrageurs attempt to make a profit by simultaneously entering into several transactions in multiple markets in an effort to benefit from price discrepancies across these markets.

SEVERAL FACTORS HAVE CAUSED CHANGES IN THE ENERGY MARKETS, POTENTIALLY AFFECTING ENERGY PRICES

The physical markets for energy commodities underwent change and turmoil from 2002 through 2006, which affected prices in the spot and futures markets. We reported that numerous changes in both the physical and futures markets may have affected energy prices. However, because these changes occurred simultaneously, identifying the specific effect of any one of these changes on energy prices is difficult.

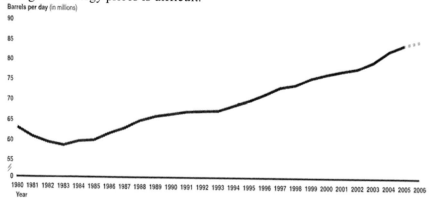

Figure 1. Increase in World Demand for Crude Oil (Actual and Estimated), 1980–2006

Source: GAO analysis of EIA data.

Note: The world oil demand data for 2006 represent a preliminary estimate.

Various Changes in the Physical Market Contributed to Rising Prices

The physical energy markets have undergone substantial change and turmoil during this period, which can affect spot and futures markets. Like many others, we found that a number of fundamental supply and demand conditions can affect prices. According to the Energy Information Administration (EIA), world oil demand has grown since 1983 from a low of about 59 million barrels per day in 1983 to more than 85 million barrels per day in 2006 (Figure 1). While the United States accounts for about a quarter of this demand, rapid economic growth in Asia also has stimulated a strong demand for energy commodities. For example, EIA data show that during this time frame, China's average daily demand for crude oil increased almost fourfold.

The growth in demand does not, by itself, lead to higher prices for crude oil or any other energy commodity. For example, if the growth in demand were exceeded by a growth in supply, prices would fall, other things remaining constant. However, according to EIA, the growth in demand outpaced the growth in supply, even with spare production capacity included in supply. Spare production capacity is surplus oil that can be produced and brought to the market relatively quickly to rebalance the market if there is a supply disruption anywhere in the world oil market. As shown in Figure 2, EIA estimates that global spare production capacity in 2006 was about 1.3 million barrels per day, compared with spare capability of about 10 million barrels per day in the mid-1980s and about 5.6 million barrels a day as recently as 2002.

Major weather and political events also can lead to supply disruptions and higher prices. In its analysis, EIA has cited the following examples:

- Hurricanes Katrina and Rita removed about 450,000 barrels per day from the world oil market from June 2005 to June 2006.
- Instability in major oil-producing countries of the Organization of Petroleum Exporting Countries (OPEC), such as Iran, Iraq, and Nigeria, have lowered production in some cases and increased the risk of future production shortfalls in others.
- Oil production in Russia, a major driver of non-OPEC supply growth during the early 2000s, was adversely affected by a

worsened investment climate as the government raised export and
extraction taxes.

The supply of crude oil affects the supply of gasoline and heating oil, and
just as production capacity affects the supply of crude oil, refining capacity
affects the supply of those products distilled from crude oil. As we have
reported, refining capacity in the United States has not expanded at the same
pace as the demand for gasoline.[4] Inventory, another factor affecting supplies
and therefore prices, is particularly crucial to the supply and demand balance,
because it can provide a cushion against price spikes if, for example,
production is temporarily disrupted by a refinery outage or other event. Trends
toward lower levels of inventory may reduce the costs of producing gasoline,
but such trends also may cause prices to be more volatile. That is, when a
supply disruption occurs or there is an increase in demand, there are fewer
stocks of readily available gasoline to draw on, putting upward pressure on
prices.

Another consideration is that the value of the U.S. dollar on open currency
markets could affect crude oil prices. For example, because crude oil is
typically denominated in U.S. dollars, the payments that oil-producing
countries receive for their oil also are denominated in U.S. dollars. As a result,
a weak U.S. dollar decreases the value of the oil sold at a given price, and oil-
producing countries may wish to increase prices for their crude oil in order to
maintain the purchasing power in the face of a weakening U.S. dollar to the
extent they can.

The Effect on Prices of Relatively High but Falling Volatility and a Growing Volume of Trading in Derivatives Is Unclear

As you can see, conditions in the physical markets have undergone
changes that can help explain at least some of the increases in both physical
and derivatives commodity prices. As we have previously reported, futures
prices typically reflect the effects of world events on the price of the
underlying commodity such as crude oil.[5] For example, political instability and
terrorist acts in countries that supply oil create uncertainties about future
supplies, which are reflected in futures prices. Conversely, news about a new
oil discovery that would increase world oil supply could result in lower futures
prices. In other words, changes in the physical markets influence futures
prices.

Barrels per day (in millions)

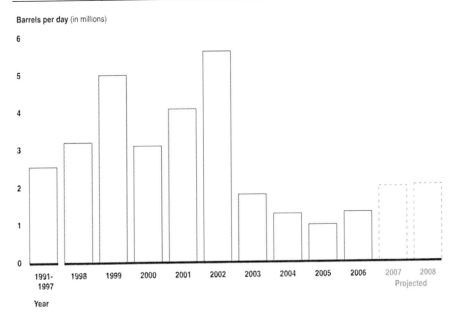

Figure 2. Estimates of World Oil Spare Production Capacity, 1991–2008

Source: GAO analysis of EIA data.

At the same time that physical markets were undergoing changes, we found that financial markets also were amidst change and evolution. For example, the annual historical volatilities between 2000 and 2006—measured using the relative change in daily prices of energy futures—generally were above or near their long-term averages, although crude oil and heating oil declined below the average and gasoline declined slightly at the end of that period. We also found that the annual volatility of natural gas fluctuated more widely than that of the other three commodities and increased in 2006 even though prices largely declined from the levels reached in 2005. Although higher volatility is often equated with higher prices, this pattern illustrates that an increase in volatility does not necessarily mean that price levels will increase. In other words, price volatility measures the variability of prices rather than the direction of the price changes.

Elsewhere in the futures market, we found an increase in the number of noncommercial traders such as managed money traders.[6] Attracted in part by the trends in prices and volatility, a growing number of traders sought opportunities to hedge against those changes or profit from them. Using CFTC's large trader data, we found that from July 2003 to December 2006, crude oil futures and options contracts experienced the most dramatic increase, with the average number of noncommercial traders more than doubling from about 125 to about 286. As shown in Figure 3, while the growth was less dramatic in the other commodities, the average number of noncommercial traders also showed an upward trend for unleaded gasoline, heating oil, and natural gas.

Not surprisingly, our work also revealed that as the number of traders increased, so did the trading volume on NYMEX for all energy futures contracts, particularly crude oil and natural gas. Average daily contract volume for crude oil increased by 90 percent from 2001 through 2006, and natural gas increased by just over 90 percent. Unleaded gasoline and heating oil experienced less dramatic growth in their trading volumes over this period.

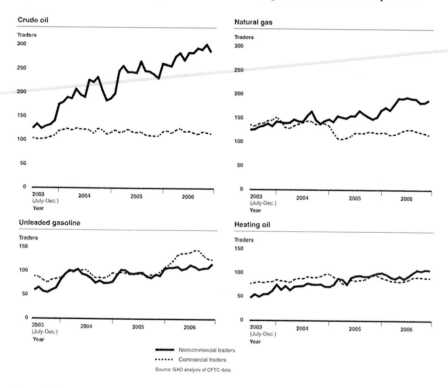

Figure 3. Average Daily Number of Large Commercial and Noncommercial Traders per Month, July 2003–December 2006 TradersCrude

Source: GAO analysis of CFTC data.

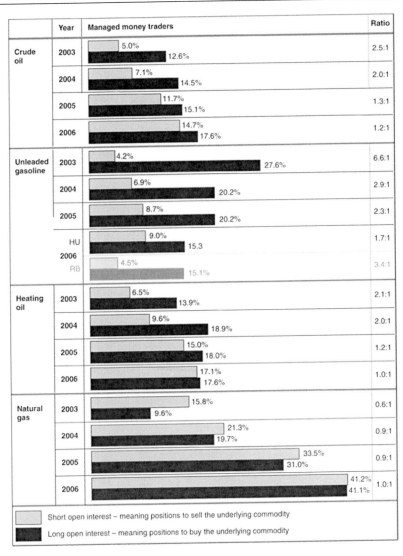

Figure 4. Percentage of Long and Short Open Interest in Futures and Options for Managed Money Traders, July 2003–December 2006

Source: GAO analysis of CFTC data.
Note: Data for 2003 were for July through December. The percentages indicate what portion of long and short open interest was held by managed money traders. For example, in 2004, managed money traders held 14.5 percent of the total long open interest for crude oil and 7.1 percent of the total short open interest. Because data are not included for all categories of traders, the percentages for these three categories within a particular period do not total 100. These data should be viewed as a general overview of managed money traders' positions. They do not provide insights into how traders' individual positions changed over time. Our data for 2006 include contract trading data for NYMEX reformulated gasoline blendstock (RB) and for the NYMEX gasoline contract (HU) that began to replace RB.

While much harder to quantify, another notable trend was the significant increase in the amount of energy derivatives traded outside exchanges. Trading in these markets is much less transparent, and comprehensive data are not available because these energy markets are not regulated. However, using the Bank for International Settlements data as a rough proxy for trends in the trading volume of OTC energy derivatives, the face value or notional amounts outstanding of OTC commodity derivatives excluding precious metals, such as gold, grew from December 2001 to December 2005 by more than 850 percent to over $3.2 trillion.[7]

Further, while some market observers believe that managed money traders were exerting upward pressure on prices by predominantly buying futures contracts, CFTC data we analyzed revealed that from the middle of 2003 through the end of 2006, the trading activity of managed money participants became increasingly balanced between buying (those that expect prices to go up) and selling (those that expect prices to go down). Using CFTC large trader reporting data, we found that from July 2003 through December 2006, managed money traders' ratio of buying (long) to selling (short) open interest positions was 2.5:1 indicating that on the whole, this category of participants was 2.5 times as likely to expect prices to rise as opposed to fall throughout that period, which they did. However, as Figure 4 illustrates, by 2006, this ratio fell to 1.2:1, suggesting that managed money traders as a whole were more evenly divided in their expectations about future prices. As you can see, managed money trading in unleaded gasoline, heating oil, and natural gas showed similar trends.

Overall, we found that views were mixed about whether these trends put any upward pressure on prices. Some market participants and observers have concluded that large purchases of oil futures contracts by speculators could have created an additional demand for oil that could lead to higher prices. Conversely, some federal agencies and other market observers took the position that speculative trading activity did not have a significant impact on prices. For example, an April 2005 CFTC study of the markets concluded that increased trading by speculative traders, including hedge funds, did not lead to higher energy prices or volatility. This study also argued that hedge funds provided increased liquidity to the market and dampened volatility. Still others told us that while speculative trading in the futures market could contribute to short-term price movements in the physical markets, they did not believe it was possible to sustain a speculative "bubble" over time, because the two markets were linked and both responded to information about changes in supply and demand caused by such factors as the weather or geographical events. In the view of these observers and market participants, speculation could not lead to artificially high or low prices over a long period.

CFTC OVERSEES EXCHANGES AND HAS LIMITED AUTHORITY OVER OTHER DERIVATIVES MARKETS

Under CEA, CFTC's authority for protecting market users from fraudulent, manipulative, and abusive practices in energy derivatives trading is primarily focused on the operations of traditional futures exchanges, such as NYMEX, where energy futures are traded. Off exchange markets, which are available only to eligible traders of certain commodities under specified conditions, are not regulated, although CFTC may enforce antimanipulation and antfraud provisions of the CEA with respect to trading in those markets. The growth in trading off exchange has raised questions about the sufficiency of CFTC's limited authority over these markets. These changes and innovations also have brought into question the methods CFTC uses to categorize published data about futures trading by participants in the off exchange markets and whether information about their activities in off exchange markets would be useful to the public. CFTC is taking steps to better understand these issues. Most importantly, it is currently examining the relationship between trading in the regulated and exempt energy markets and the role this trading plays in the price discovery process. It is also examining the sufficiency of the scope of its authority over these markets—an issue that will warrant further examination as part of the CFTC reauthorization process.

CFTC has General Oversight Authority over Futures Exchanges, but Information on These Exchanges Reported to the Public Has Not Kept Pace with Changing Market Conditions

To help provide transparency in the markets, CFTC provides the public information on open interest in exchange-traded futures and options by commercial and noncommercial traders for various commodities in its weekly Commitment of Traders (COT) reports.[8] As we reported, CFTC observed that the exchange-traded derivatives markets, as well as trading patterns and practices, have evolved. In 2006, CFTC initiated a comprehensive review of the COT reporting program out of concern that the reports in their present form might not accurately reflect the commercial or noncommercial nature of positions held by nontraditional hedgers, such as swaps dealers.[9] A disconnect between the classifications and evolving trading activity could distort the accuracy and relevance of reported information to users and the public, thereby limiting its usefulness for both.

In December 2006, CFTC announced a 2-year pilot program for publishing a supplemental COT report that includes positions of commodity index traders in a separate category. However, the pilot does not include any energy commodities. Although commodity index traders are active in energy markets, according to CFTC officials, currently available data would not permit an accurate breakout of index trading in these markets. For example, some traders, such as commodity index pools, use the futures markets to hedge commodity index positions they hold in the OTC market. However, these traders also may have positions in the physical markets, which means the reports that CTFC receives on market activities, which do not include such off-exchange transactions, may not present an accurate picture of all positions in the market place for the commodity. In response to our recommendation to reexamine the COT classifications for energy markets, CFTC agreed to explore whether the classifications should be refined to improve their accuracy and relevance.

CFTC Authority over Exempt Commercial Markets and OTC Markets is Limited, and Views Vary about the Sufficiency of Its Regulatory Authority with Respect to Off-Exchange Energy Derivatives

Now let me address some of the larger policy issues associated with CFTC's oversight of these markets. Under CEA, CFTC's authority for protecting market users from fraudulent, manipulative, and abusive practices in energy derivatives trading is primarily focused on the operations of traditional futures exchanges, such as NYMEX, where energy futures are traded. Currently, CFTC receives limited information on derivatives trading on exempt commercial markets—for example, records of allegations or complaints of suspected fraud or manipulation, and price, quantity, and other data on contracts that average five or more trades a day. The agency may receive limited information, such as trading records, from OTC participants to help CFTC enforce the CEA's antifraud or antimanipulation provisions. The scope of CFTC's oversight authority has raised concerns among some members of Congress and others that activities on these markets are largely unregulated, and that additional CFTC oversight is needed.

While some observers have called for more oversight of OTC derivatives, most notably for CFTC to be given greater oversight authority of this market, others oppose any such action. Supporters of more CFTC oversight authority believe that regulation of OTC derivatives markets is necessary to protect the regulated markets and consumers from potential abuse and possible manipulation. One of their concerns is that, due to the lack of complete information on the size of this market or the terms of the contracts, CFTC may not be assured that trading on the OTC market is not adversely affecting the regulated markets and, ultimately, consumers. However others, including the President's Working Group, have concluded that OTC derivatives generally are not subject to manipulation because contracts are settled in cash on the basis of a rate or price determined in a separate, highly liquid market that does not serve a significant price discovery function.[10] The Working Group also noted that if electronic markets were to develop and serve a price discovery function, then consideration should be given to enacting a limited regulatory regime aimed at enhancing market transparency and efficiency through CFTC, as the regulator of exchange-traded derivatives.

However, the lack of reported data about this market makes addressing concerns about its function and effect on regulated markets and entities challenging. In a June 2007 *Federal Register* release clarifying its large trader reporting authority, CFTC noted that having data about the off-exchange positions of traders with large positions on regulated futures exchanges could enhance the commission's ability to deter and prevent price manipulation or other disruptions to the integrity of the regulated futures markets.[11] According to CFTC officials, the commission has proposed amendments to clarify its authority under the CEA to collect information and bring fraud actions in principal-to-principal transactions in these markets, enhancing CFTC's ability to enforce antifraud provisions of the CEA.[12]

Also, in September 2007, CFTC conducted a hearing to begin examining trading on regulated exchanges and exempt commercial markets more closely. The hearing focused on a number of issues, including

- the current tiered regulatory approach established by the Commodity Futures Modernization Act, which amended the CEA, and whether this model is beneficial;

- the similarities and differences between exempt commercial markets and regulated exchanges, and the associated regulatory risks of each market; and
- the types of regulatory or legislative changes that might be appropriate to address any identified risks.

Given ongoing questions about the similarity of products traded on the markets and how and whether exempt markets play a role in the price discovery process and whether existing reporting requirements are sufficient, we recommend that Congress take up this issue during the CFTC reauthorization process to begin to answer some of these questions and the implications for the current regulatory structure in light of the changes that have occurred in this market.

CFTC ENGAGES IN LARGE TRADER REPORTING, SURVEILLANCE, AND ENFORCEMENT ACTIVITIES, BUT THE EFFECTIVENESS OF THE ACTIVITIES IS LARGELY UNCERTAIN

CFTC provides oversight for commodity futures markets by analyzing large trader reporting data, conducting routine surveillance, and investigating and taking enforcement actions against market participants and others. The commission uses information gathered from surveillance activities to identify unusual trading activity and possible market abuse. In particular, CFTC's large trader reporting system (LTRS) provides essential information on the majority of all trading activity on futures exchanges. CFTC staff said they routinely investigate traders with large open positions, but do not routinely maintain information about such inquiries, thereby making it difficult to determine the usefulness and extent of these activities. According to recent data provided by CFTC, about 10 percent of the enforcement actions involved energy-related commodities. However, as with programs operating in regulatory environments where performance is not easily measurable, evaluating the effectiveness of CFTC's enforcement activities is challenging because it lacks effective outcome-based performance measures.

CFTC Oversight Includes Surveillance of Energy Futures Trading, but the Full Extent of Follow-up Activities Is Uncertain

CFTC conducts regular market surveillance and oversight of energy trading on NYMEX and other futures exchanges, focusing on detecting and preventing disruptive practices before they occur and keeping the CFTC commissioners informed of possible manipulation or abuse. According to CFTC staff, when a potential market problem has been identified, surveillance staff generally contact the exchange or traders for more information. To confirm positions and determine intent, staff may question exchange employees, brokers, or traders. According to the staff, CFTC's Division of Market Oversight may issue a warning letter or make a referral to the Division of Enforcement to conduct a nonpublic investigation into the trading activity. Markets where surveillance problems have not been resolved may be included in reports presented to the commission at weekly surveillance meetings.

According to CFTC staff, they routinely make inquiries about traders with large open positions approaching expiration, but formal records of their findings are only kept in cases with evidence of improper trading. If LTRS data revealed that a trader had a large open market position that could disrupt markets if it were not closed before expiration, CFTC staff would contact the trader to determine why the trader had the position and what plans the trader had to close the position before expiration or ensure that the trader was able to take delivery. If the trader provided a reasonable explanation for the position and a reasonable delivery or liquidation strategy, staff said no further action would be required. CFTC staff said they would document such contacts on the basis of their importance in either informal notes, e-mails to supervisors, or informal memorandums. According to one CFTC official, no formal record would be made unless some signal indicated improper trading activity. However, without such data, CFTC's measures of the effectiveness of its actions to combat fraud and manipulation in the markets would not reflect all surveillance activity, and CFTC management might miss opportunities to identify trends in activities or markets and better target its limited resources. In response to our recommendation, CFTC agreed to improve its documentation of its surveillance activities.

CFTC Energy-Related Enforcement Actions Generally involved Allegations of False Reporting and Attempted Manipulation, but its Program Received a Mixed Rating and Lacks Effective Outcome-Based Performance Measures

CFTC's Division of Enforcement is charged with enforcing the antimanipulation sections of the CEA.[13] The enforcement actions CFTC has taken in its energy-related cases generally have involved false public reporting as a method of attempting to manipulate prices on both the NYMEX futures market and the off-exchange markets. CFTC officials said that from October 2000 to September 2005, the agency initiated 287 enforcement cases and more than 30 of these cases involved energy trading. In the past several months, CFTC has taken a series of actions involving energy commodities, including allegations of false reporting, attempted manipulation of NYMEX natural gas futures prices, and attempted manipulation of physical natural gas prices.

Although CFTC has undertaken enforcement actions and levied fines, measuring the effectiveness of these activities is an ongoing challenge. For example, the Office of Management and Budget's most recent 2004 Program Assessment Rating Tool (PART) assessment of the CFTC enforcement program identified a number of limitations of CFTC's performance measures.[14] As is the case with most enforcement programs, identifying outcome-oriented performance measures can be particularly challenging.[15] However, as we point out in the report, there are a number of other ways to evaluate program effectiveness, such as using expert panel reviews, customer service surveys, and process and outcome evaluations. We have found with other programs that the form of the evaluations reflects differences in program structure and anticipated outcomes, and that the evaluations are designed around the programs and what they aim to achieve.[16] Without utilizing these or other methods to evaluate program effectiveness, CFTC is unable to demonstrate whether its enforcement program is meeting its overall objectives. CFTC has agreed that this is a matter that should be examined and has included development of measures to evaluate its effectiveness in its strategic plan and has requested funding to study the feasibility of developing more meaningful measures.

In closing, I would like to reemphasize the difficulty in attributing increased energy prices to any one of the numerous changes in the physical or derivatives markets. As I have mentioned, our research shows that the physical and derivatives markets have both undergone substantial change and evolution, and market participant and regulatory views were mixed about the extent to which these developments exerted upward pressure on prices. Because of the importance of understanding the potential effects of such developments in these markets, ongoing review and analysis are warranted. As the scope of CFTC's authority is debated, additional information is needed to understand what may need to be done to best protect investors from fraudulent, manipulative, and abusive practices. Such information includes

- how different or similar are the characteristics and uses of exchange and off-exchange products being traded and do these continue to justify different regulatory treatment;
- to what extent does trading in off-exchange financial derivatives affect price discovery and what are the regulatory and policy implications;
- how large of an effect are nontraditional market participants, such as commodity index funds, having in these markets; and
- are the changes in the energy markets unique or are such concerns also worth reviewing for other commodity markets.

By answering questions such as these, CFTC and the Congress will be better positioned to determine what changes, if any, may be needed to oversee these markets.

Mr. Chairman, this concludes my prepared statement. I would be happy to respond to any questions that you or other members of the subcommittee might have.

End Notes

[1] GAO, *Commodity Futures Trading Commission: Trends in Energy Derivatives Markets Raise Questions about CFTC's Oversight*, GAO-08-25 (Washington, D.C.: Oct. 19, 2007).

[2] Our analysis of energy prices and energy financial markets is generally limited to the time period from January 2002 through December 2006.

[3] Energy swap transactions also may be conducted off-exchange if they satisfy the requirements for excluded swap transactions contained in section 2(g) of the Commodity Exchange Act.

[4] GAO, *Motor Fuels: Understanding the Factors That Influence the Retail Price of Gasoline*, GAO-05-525SP (Washington, D.C.: May 2005).

[5] GAO-05-525SP.

[6] CFTC collects data on traders holding positions at or above specific reporting levels set by the Commission. This information is collected as part of CFTC's large trader reporting system.

[7] The Bank for International Settlements is an international organization that fosters international monetary and financial cooperation and serves as a bank for central banks.

[8] These reports include the number of traders, changes since the last report, and open positions.

[9] 71 Fed. Reg. 35627, 35630-31 (June 21, 2006).

[10] President's Working Group on Financial Markets, *Over-the-Counter Derivatives Markets and the Commodity Exchange Act* (Nov. 9, 1999). Members of group are the Chairman of CFTC, the Secretary of the Treasury, the Chairman of the Board of Governors of the Federal Reserve, and the Chairman of the Securities and Exchange Commission.

[11] As stated by CFTC, the purpose of the proposed regulation is to make it explicit that persons holding or controlling reportable positions on a reporting market must retain books and records and make available to the commission upon request any pertinent information with respect to all other positions and transactions in the commodity in which the trader has a reportable position, including positions held or controlled or transactions executed over-the-counter or pursuant to sections 2(d), 2(g) or 2(h)(1)–(2) of the CEA or part 35 of the commission's regulations, on exempt commercial markets operating pursuant to sections 2(h)(3)–(5) of the CEA, on exempt boards of trade operating pursuant to Section 5d of the CEA, and on foreign boards of trade (hereinafter referred to collectively as non-reporting transactions); and to make the regulation clearer and more complete with respect to hedging activity. The purpose of the amendments is to clarify CFTC's regulatory reporting requirements for such traders. 72 Fed. Reg. 34413..

[12] Section 4b of the CEA is CFTC's main antifraud authority. In a November 2000 decision, the 7th Circuit Court of Appeals ruled that CFTC only could use section 4b in intermediated transactions—those involving a broker. *Commodity Trend Service, Inc. v. CFTC*, 233 F.3d 981, 991-992 (7th Cir. 2000). As amended by the Commodity Futures Modernization Act of 2000, the CEA permits off-exchange futures and options transactions that are done on a principal-to-principal basis, such as energy transactions pursuant to CEA sections 2(h)(1) and 2(h)(3). According to CFTC, House and Senate CFTC reauthorization bills introduced during the 109th Congress (H.R. 4473 and S. 1566) would have amended section 4b to clarify that Congress intends for CFTC to enforce section 4b in connection with off-exchange principal-to-principal futures transactions, including exempt commodity transactions in energy under section 2(h) as well as all transactions conducted on derivatives transaction execution facilities.

[13] Section 9(a)(2) of the CEA prohibits "(a)ny person to manipulate or attempt to manipulate the price of any commodity in interstate commerce, or for future delivery on or subject to the rules of any registered entity, or to corner or attempt to corner any such commodity or knowingly to deliver or cause to be delivered for transmission through the mails or interstate commerce by telegraph, telephone, wireless, or other means of communication false or misleading or knowingly inaccurate reports concerning crop or market information or conditions that affect or tend to affect the price of any commodity interstate commerce...."

[14] The assessment includes a series of questions meant to serve as a diagnostic performance tool, drawing on available program performance and evaluation information to form conclusions about program benefits and recommend adjustments that may improve results.

[15] GAO, *Results Oriented Government: GPRA Has Established a Solid Foundation for Achieving Greater Results*, GAO-04-594T (Washington, D.C.: Mar. 31, 2004).

[16] GAO, *Program Evaluation: OMB's PART Reviews Increased Agencies' Attention to Improving Evidence of Program Results*, GAO-06-67 (Washington, D.C.: Oct. 28, 2005).

CHAPTER SOURCES

The following chapters have been previously published:

Chapter 1 - This is an edited, reformatted and augmented version of a Congressional Research Service publication, Report Order Code RL34555, updated July 8, 2008.

Chapter 2 – These remarks were delivered as testimony given on October 24, 2007. Orice M. Williams, Director, Financial Markets and Community Investment, before the Subcommittee on General Farm Commodities and Risk Management, Committee on Agriculture, House of Representatvies.

Chapter 3 – This is an edited, reformatted and augmented version of a Congressional Research Service publication, Report Order Code RL21401, update June 9, 2008.

Chapter 4 – This is an edited, reformatted and augmented version of a United States Government Accountability Office publication, Report GAO-08-25, dated October 2007.

INDEX

A

abusive, viii, 25, 26, 28, 29, 36, 69, 70, 72, 79, 84, 103, 113, 125, 126, 131
academic, 27, 45, 79, 114
accountability, 6, 8, 9, 13, 14, 15, 16, 17, 18, 62, 70, 71, 82
accuracy, 28, 30, 53, 54, 74, 126
acquisitions, 69
adjudication, 85, 87
administrative, 100
advocacy, 44
AEP, 91
agricultural, 5, 6, 16, 19, 32, 53, 73, 90, 96, 107, 108, 110
agricultural commodities, 6, 19, 53, 73, 107
aid, 12
air, 43, 51
air quality, 43
alternatives, 39, 114
amendments, 60, 99, 127, 132
analysts, 2, 3, 55, 79, 80, 108
annual review, 86
anticompetitive, 17, 69
appendix, 30
application, 51, 62
appropriations, 11, 14, 15, 19

arbitrage, 35
argument, 4, 6, 56
Asia, 40, 119
asian, 40
assessment, 50, 57, 65, 68, 69, 70, 71, 80, 100, 130, 132
assets, 5, 14, 32, 81, 96
assumptions, 3
auditing, 27, 114
availability, 56
averaging, 56

B

banking, 53, 59
banks, 5, 22, 27, 45, 55, 59, 79, 98, 115, 118, 131
base year, 97
behavior, 69, 70
benefits, 1, 69, 132
blends, 43
board of governors, 59, 66, 97, 132
bonds, 8, 105, 110
boutique fuels, 43
brokerage, 21
brothers, 3

BTUs, 85
bubble, 2, 4, 8, 21, 46, 108, 110, 124
Bureau of Economic Analysis, 78
buses, vii, 23, 80
bust, 21
butyl ether, 43
buyer, 21, 80, 82

C

case law, 100
cash flow, 22
causality, 72
central bank, 98, 131
certification, 51
chaos, 105
Chicago Mercantile Exchange, 84
classes, 106
classification, 53
Clean Air Act, 43
clients, 96
collusion, 69
commerce, 21, 100, 132
commercial bank, 59
commercials, 54
Committee on Homeland Security, 22, 45, 79, 98
Committee on Oversight and Government Reform, 76
Committee on the Judiciary, 17
commodity futures, 18, 36, 51, 53, 54, 61, 69, 96, 128
Commodity Futures Trading Commission (CFTC), v, vii, 2, 16, 20, 22, 23, 26, 74, 78, 81, 87, 92, 95, 96, 99, 103, 104, 111, 113, 131
commodity markets, 2, 9, 131
communication, 100, 132
community, 11
competition, 36
compliance, 51, 62, 66, 85, 91, 98
composition, 4

Comptroller of the Currency, 59
concentration, 12
conception, 110
confidence, 15, 59
congestion, 63
congress, iv, 6, 8, 13, 14, 16, 24, 26, 29, 30, 72, 73, 99, 103, 105, 106, 107, 108, 109, 112, 116, 127, 128, 131, 132
consensus, 43
conspiracy, 69
consultants, 27
consumers, 13, 19, 25, 33, 43, 59, 71, 97, 117, 127
consumption, 3, 40, 43
contract prices, 45
control, 5, 16
convergence, 35
copper, 3
corporations, 97
cost-effective, 71
costs, 4, 10, 21, 33, 43, 97, 109, 120
counsel, 85
Court of Appeals, 99, 132
credit, 97
CTA, 34
currency, 41, 96, 120
current prices, 1, 8
customers, 7, 22, 26, 51, 70, 71, 82, 83, 84, 99, 104

D

database, 26, 62
decisions, 2, 3, 8, 19, 44, 72, 73, 85, 100
defendants, 67, 68, 99
definition, 9, 10, 14, 36, 96, 110
deflation, 78
delivery, 7, 12, 13, 14, 15, 16, 18, 20, 21, 25, 28, 31, 32, 33, 34, 35, 37, 43, 58, 63, 64, 65, 67, 80, 81, 96, 97, 100, 105, 116, 117, 129, 132
Department of Agriculture, 68

Department of Energy, 27, 78
Department of Justice(DOJ), 17, 27, 91
detection, vii, 23, 26, 111, 113
deviation, 98
diesel fuel, 13
directives, 82
disclosure, 107
discovery, 96
dispersion, 98
division, 67, 83
draft, 30, 74, 96

E

economic fundamentals, 2
economic growth, 40, 119
electrical power, 108
electricity, 59, 66, 108
emission, 57
employees, 11, 14, 18, 19, 64, 129
Energy Information Administration (EIA), 27, 78, 119
energy markets, viii, 4, 6, 11, 13, 14, 19, 22, 25, 26, 27, 48, 54, 55, 64, 71, 79, 103, 107, 110, 111, 113, 114, 115, 119, 124, 125, 126, 131
Energy Policy Act, 66
Energy Policy Act of 2005, 66
energy supply, 40
Enron, vii, 5, 6, 12, 16, 67, 68, 90, 103, 107, 108
Enron Corp., vii, 103
environment, 71
equity, 83
ethanol, 43
evolution, 71, 121, 131
exchange markets, 6, 26, 67, 72, 125, 130
exchange-based trading, 61
execution, 97, 99, 132
exposure, 54, 82, 104
expulsion, 85
extraction, 42, 120

F

failure, viii, 85, 103
Farm Bill, 6, 12, 103
fear, vii
Federal Energy Regulatory Commission (FERC), 14, 27, 29, 45, 59, 66, 68, 79, 91, 100
federal register, 53, 60, 80, 110, 127
federal reserve, 21, 59, 66, 79, 97, 106, 132
Federal Reserve Bank, 66
Federal Trade Commission (FTC), 25, 27, 35, 50, 51, 59, 60, 61, 66, 68, 69, 88, 99, 112, 113, 130, 132
fees, 21
felony, 100
finance, 79
financial institution, 5, 99, 104
financial markets, 8, 28, 31, 32, 33, 39, 96, 105, 110, 116, 121, 131
Financial Services Authority (FSA), 7, 8, 11, 69, 81
financial soundness, 36
fines, 29, 67, 69, 85, 108, 130
firms, 36, 45, 51, 62, 63, 67, 83, 96, 104, 108, 110
flood, 110
fluctuations, 11, 16, 20, 31, 33, 100, 117
focusing, 62, 129
forecasting, vii, 1, 3, 33, 117
foreign exchange, 13
fraud, 6, 12, 26, 28, 36, 56, 60, 61, 65, 69, 73, 100, 104, 106, 126, 127, 129
freight, 57
fuel, 33
funding, 130
funds, 2, 4, 8, 9, 14, 15, 18, 21, 24, 25, 27, 28, 34, 36, 45, 51, 54, 59, 70, 71, 79, 96, 104, 110, 112, 113, 114, 115, 118, 124, 131

G

gambling, 1

gasoline, vii, 13, 23, 24, 25, 26, 27, 28, 31, 32, 33, 34, 39, 42, 43, 44, 45, 47, 48, 49, 52, 63, 78, 96, 97, 104, 111, 114, 116, 117, 120, 121, 122, 123, 124

global demand, 27, 39, 41, 71, 112, 114

global economy, 40

global insight, 37

goals, 25, 30, 51, 70, 71, 74, 113

gold, 48, 124

government, iv, viii, 5, 27, 42, 70, 79, 91, 103, 104, 105, 114, 120

Government Accountability Office, v, 6, 22, 23, 133

grand jury, 84

gross domestic product, 78

groups, 26

growth, 2, 6, 24, 26, 40, 41, 42, 43, 48, 57, 58, 70, 71, 72, 113, 115, 119, 122, 125

guidance, 98

guilty, 69

H

handling, 6, 104

hearing, 29, 50, 57, 60, 80, 82, 85, 86, 87, 127

heating, vii, 13, 23, 24, 25, 26, 27, 28, 31, 32, 34, 39, 42, 44, 45, 47, 48, 49, 63, 78, 97, 104, 111, 114, 117, 120, 121, 122, 124

heating oil, vii, 13, 23, 24, 25, 26, 27, 28, 31, 32, 34, 39, 42, 44, 45, 47, 48, 49, 63, 78, 97, 104, 111, 114, 117, 120, 121, 122, 124

hedge funds, 2, 24, 25, 27, 28, 34, 36, 45, 54, 59, 79, 110, 112, 113, 114, 115, 118, 124

hedging, 14, 18, 54, 60, 80, 99, 132

hiring, 18

homeland security, 75

house, viii, 11, 12, 13, 14, 15, 16, 75, 76, 77, 78, 99, 112, 132, 133

hub, 31, 116

hurricanes, 35

hybrid, 104

I

incentive, 9, 10

incidence, 4

income, 104

indices, 22, 54

industrial, 9

industry, 36, 40, 43, 55, 58, 61, 63, 66, 73, 79, 80, 82, 104, 105, 106

inelastic, 31

inflation, 28, 78, 97

infrastructure, 15

initiation, 53, 96

injury, iv

innovation, 28, 36

insecurity, 40

Inspector General, 15, 27, 70, 80

instability, 7, 40, 44

in-state, 108

institutions, 2, 4

instruments, 35, 59, 105

integrity, 26, 36, 50, 51, 60, 71, 72, 114, 127

IntercontinentalExchange (ICE), 6, 7, 8, 22, 49, 56, 57, 58, 63, 79, 81, 98, 99, 109

interest rates, 105, 106

intermediaries, 37, 51

internal controls, 106

International Monetary Fund, 99

international standards, 11

interstate, 59, 66, 100, 132

interstate commerce, 100, 132

interview, 79

intrastate, 91

inventories, 31, 43

Investigations, viii, 45, 75, 79, 98, 103, 108

investigative, 84
investment, 2, 3, 4, 5, 8, 9, 20, 21, 22, 25,
    27, 33, 39, 42, 45, 54, 59, 79, 96, 114,
    115, 117, 118, 120
investment bank, 3, 5, 22, 27, 45, 54, 59,
    79, 115, 118
investors, 2, 4, 5, 7, 8, 10, 11, 18, 21, 22, 36,
    54, 72, 104, 106, 110, 131
isolation, 44
ISS, 62, 63

J

joint demand, 45
judge, 87
jurisdiction, 5, 15, 16, 18, 20, 26, 35, 66, 97,
    104, 105, 106, 107
jury, 84, 87

K

Katrina, 42, 119

L

law, 6, 7, 14, 15, 16, 17, 18, 26, 56, 59, 69,
    99, 100, 104, 105, 107
leadership, 36
legality, 35, 107
legislation, 5, 6, 11, 35, 104, 106, 107
legislative proposals, 2, 9
limitations, 130
liquidate, 9, 14, 18
liquidation, 11, 64, 65, 129
liquidity, 33, 45, 118, 124
litigation, 88, 89
LNG, ii
loans, 22
location, 32, 80, 81, 116, 117
long period, 28, 46, 125
losses, 9, 10, 21

M

magnetic, iv
maintenance, 21
management, 5, 29, 53, 65, 70, 129
mandates, 104
market disruption, 63
market position, 63, 65, 66, 88, 110, 129
market prices, 33, 35, 50, 55, 56, 100, 114,
    117
marketing, 108
marketplace, 31, 44, 62, 104, 106, 107
maximum price, 83
measurement, 33
measures, 24, 25, 30, 33, 45, 61, 65, 69, 70,
    71, 73, 74, 98, 110, 112, 113, 116, 121,
    128, 129, 130
membership, 79, 85
memorandum of understanding, 8, 66, 68
mergers, 69
messengers, 2
metals, 6, 22, 48, 54, 57, 78, 83, 124
methyl tertiary, 43
million barrels per day, 40, 41, 119
misleading, 100, 132
money, 2, 8, 9, 10, 33, 34, 39, 45, 47, 49,
    52, 53, 96, 97, 109, 110, 114, 117, 121,
    123, 124
morning, 62
mortgage, 110

N

nation, 69
natural disasters, 40
negotiation, 59
network, 5, 12, 62, 109
New York Mercantile Exchange, 8, 11, 24,
    26, 78, 81, 82, 104, 112, 114
nongovernmental, 79
normal, 25

O

obligation, 20, 21, 28, 31, 32, 36, 81, 96, 97, 98, 117

off-exchange trading, 36, 54, 61, 72

Office of Management and Budget (OMB), 30, 80, 61, 69, 70, 71, 101, 130, 132

oil production, 27, 41

online, ii

opposition, 106

optimism, 8

Organization of the Petroleum Exporting Countries (OPEC), ii, 3, 40, 41, 42, 97, 119

oversight, viii, 7, 24, 26, 27, 29, 36, 49, 50, 51, 55, 57, 59, 61, 62, 66, 72, 73, 74, 80, 97, 98, 103, 107, 112, 113, 115, 116, 126, 127, 128, 129

over-the-counter, vii, 5, 12, 13, 24, 78, 80, 99, 103, 104, 112, 114, 132

P

PART, 69, 71, 80, 100, 101, 130, 132

partnerships, 97

passive, 14, 19

penalties, 12, 36, 68, 88, 90, 91

pension, 2, 4, 8, 9, 54, 110

permit, 11, 36, 54, 126

petroleum, 17, 19, 22, 33, 40, 43, 57, 68, 95, 117, 119

petroleum products, 17, 19, 40, 43

pipeline hub, 31, 116

planning, 33, 70, 117

play, 3, 12, 103, 109, 128

police, 84

political instability, 27, 39, 40, 71, 112, 114, 120

pools, 99, 126

pork, 105

portfolio, 2, 4, 8, 9, 108

ports, 19

power, 2, 4, 11, 12, 16, 20, 42, 108, 120

power plant, 108

premium, vii, 1, 3, 4, 21, 108

pressure, 8, 25, 28, 35, 43, 45, 49, 109, 120, 124, 131

prevention, 36, 51

price changes, 1, 3, 9, 32, 33, 45, 72, 98, 104, 117, 121

price deflator, 78

price index, 2, 14

price manipulation, viii, 12, 14, 50, 51, 60, 62, 100, 103, 109, 127

price movements, 21, 33, 46, 63, 83, 108, 124

private, 43, 58, 96, 108

private investment, 96

probability, 10

producers, 1, 2, 3, 9, 19, 31, 32, 33, 34, 44, 79, 116, 117

production, 3, 24, 31, 40, 41, 42, 43, 112, 119, 120

profit, vii, 1, 3, 20, 21, 31, 33, 35, 45, 49, 96, 104, 107, 118, 121

program, 24, 25, 29, 30, 36, 53, 54, 61, 63, 64, 69, 70, 71, 73, 74, 80, 82, 87, 108, 112, 113, 115, 126, 130, 132

Program Assessment Rating Too, 69, 130

promote innovation, 36

propane, 69

property, iv, 96

protection, 19, 51

protocols, 66, 99

proxy, 48, 71, 124

public, 6, 12, 14, 15, 21, 22, 24, 25, 26, 28, 30, 36, 50, 51, 53, 55, 56, 63, 67, 69, 72, 73, 74, 79, 84, 100, 104, 105, 106, 112, 114, 115, 125, 130

public interest, 6, 70, 72, 105

public policy, 72

publishers, 66

purchasing power, 42, 120

Q

Qatar, 97
qualifications, 36, 82

R

range, 5, 27, 32, 73, 79, 88, 104, 114
ratings, 61
real estate, 110
recall, 83
record keeping, 104, 106
recordkeeping violations, 88
refineries, 28, 43, 115
refiners, vii, 9, 27, 33, 79, 117
refining, 27, 42, 114, 120
regional, 62
regular, 62, 63, 70, 129
regulation, 4, 5, 6, 7, 11, 12, 13, 14, 15, 16,
    17, 18, 19, 21, 26, 29, 36, 37, 49, 50, 51,
    70, 80, 81, 82, 83, 97, 99, 103, 104, 105,
    106, 107, 109, 127, 132
regulators, 12, 19, 29, 59, 66, 67, 72, 80,
    106, 107, 114
regulatory oversight, 49, 97
regulatory requirements, 7, 12, 14, 109
relationship, 8, 26, 29, 33, 63, 65, 68, 72,
    78, 82, 125
relevance, 28, 30, 54, 74, 126
republican, 75
residential, 110
resolution, 87
resources, 1, 3, 18, 29, 65, 69, 73, 79, 129
responsibilities, 36, 51, 82
restitution, 36
retail, 13, 26, 34, 72, 97, 99, 117
returns, 2, 4, 8, 9, 72
rice, vii
risk, 1, 2, 3, 4, 5, 8, 9, 10, 14, 18, 21, 32, 33,
    35, 42, 51, 59, 60, 61, 68, 81, 88, 96, 97,
    104, 105, 117, 118, 119, 128
risk management, 5

S

sabotage, 40
sales, 51, 66, 87, 90, 104, 105, 106
sanctions, 85, 87
scandal, 107
scores, 70
search, 72, 104
Secretary of the Treasury, 97, 132
securities, 22, 96, 105
Securities and Exchange Commission (SEC),
    27, 132
self-regulation, 36
seller, 21, 80, 82
senate, viii, 16, 17, 18, 19, 21, 22, 45, 75,
    76, 79, 98, 99, 103, 108, 132
series, 7, 69, 81, 130, 132
services, iv, 5, 97
settlements, 85
shares, 67
sharing, 8, 66, 68
Shell, 85, 88
shortage, 44
short-term, 21, 45, 124
signals, 108
silver, 3
similarity, 128
sites, 63
spare capacity, 40, 41
speculation, iv, vii, viii, 1, 2, 3, 4, 5, 6, 8, 9,
    10, 11, 12, 13, 14, 15, 16, 18, 19, 20, 21,
    28, 46, 100, 103, 109, 110, 125
spot market, 31, 32, 35, 116
staffing, 39
standard deviation, 45, 79, 98
standards, 11, 27, 43, 64, 104, 114
statutory, 5, 6, 15, 19, 32, 36, 100, 107
stock, 2, 4, 22, 106
storage, 40, 43, 44, 87, 91
strategic planning, 70
strategies, 3, 14, 19, 21, 107, 108
strength, 82

strikes, viii, 103
subpoena, 67, 99
summaries, 11
summer, 31
supervisors, 65, 129
supplemental, 11, 53, 54, 126
supply, iv, vii, 1, 2, 3, 8, 11, 16, 20, 23, 24, 25, 27, 29, 31, 34, 35, 39, 40, 41, 42, 43, 44, 45, 63, 65, 71, 79, 97, 100, 108, 110, 112, 114, 117, 119, 120, 124
supply disruption, 35, 39, 41, 42, 43, 71, 114, 119, 120
surging, 49
surplus, 41, 119
surveillance, 25, 26, 29, 30, 36, 49, 51, 61, 62, 63, 64, 65, 66, 68, 72, 73, 74, 80, 82, 83, 84, 86, 87, 104, 113, 115, 116, 128, 129
susceptibility, 51
systemic risk, 36

T

tanks, 33
targets, 70
taxes, 42, 120
technology, 44
telephone, 84, 100, 132
terminals, 7, 12, 16, 109
terrorist, 40, 44, 120
terrorist acts, 40, 44, 120
testimony, viii, 8, 67, 80, 111, 112, 133
threat, 14, 18
threatened, 112
thresholds, 56, 58, 104
time, 3, 4, 13, 20, 21, 24, 27, 30, 31, 33, 34, 39, 43, 45, 46, 47, 52, 66, 71, 72, 74, 83, 85, 99, 114, 117, 119, 121, 123, 124, 131
time frame, 21, 119
title, 97
trade, 1, 3, 8, 9, 13, 15, 18, 21, 22, 27, 28, 32, 33, 37, 47, 56, 58, 59, 64, 79, 80, 81, 82, 83, 84, 86, 87, 96, 99, 101, 104, 107, 108, 115, 117, 132
trade agreement, 22
transaction costs, 21
transfer, 96
transmission, 59, 66, 100, 132
transparency, 6, 28, 30, 34, 36, 50, 54, 60, 115, 116, 125, 127
transparent, 114, 117, 124
transportation, 8, 33, 40, 91
treasury, 66, 68, 95, 97, 105, 132
trusts, 96, 97
trustworthiness, 59

U

U.S. economy, 25
U.S. Treasury, 105
uncertainty, 33, 40, 105, 106, 107, 116, 117
United Arab Emirates, 97

V

values, 2, 31
variability, 45, 121
variable pricing, 108
variables, 106
venue, 104
volatility, 4, 10, 24, 33, 39, 44, 45, 49, 54, 78, 98, 109, 114, 117, 121, 124

W

wells, 31
wholesalers, 34, 116
winter, 35
wireless, 100, 132
written records, 30, 73, 74
wrongdoing, 70, 71, 84